BRITAIN'S BEST POLITICAL CARTOONS 2015

Dr Tim Benson is Britain's leading authority on political cartoons. He runs The Political Cartoon Gallery and Café which is located near the River Thames in Putney. He has produced numerous books on political cartoonists, including *Churchill in Caricature*, *Low and the Dictators*, *The Cartoon Century: Modern Britain through the Eyes of Its Cartoonists*, *Drawing the Curtain: The Cold War in Cartoons* and *Over the Top: A Cartoon History of Australia at War*.

BRITAIN'S BEST POLITICAL CARTOONS 2015

Edited by Tim Benson

BOOKS

1 3 5 7 9 10 8 6 4 2

Random House Books
20 Vauxhall Bridge Road
London SW1V 2SA

Random House Books is part of the Penguin Random House
group of companies whose addresses can be found
at global.penguinrandomhouse.com

This selection copyright © Tim Benson 2015
Cartoons copyright © contributing cartoonists

Tim Benson has asserted his right to be identified as the author of this Work
in accordance with the Copyright, Designs and Patents Act 1988

First published by Random House Books in 2015

www.randomhouse.co.uk

A CIP catalogue record for this book is available from the British Library

ISBN 9781847947635

Typeset in Amasis MT Light by Palimpsest Book Production Ltd, Falkirk, Stirlingshire

Printed and bound in Italy by LEGO, S.p.A.

Penguin Random House is committed to a sustainable future
for our business, our readers and our planet. This book is made from
Forest Stewardship Council® certified paper

MIX
Paper from
responsible sources
FSC® C018179
FSC
www.fsc.org

INTRODUCTION

Do **political cartoonists** really make a
difference when it comes to general elections?
The former leader of the Labour party, Neil
Kinnock, who suffered greatly at the hands of
cartoonists during his two election defeats in 1987
and 1992, certainly believed so. According to
Kinnock, 'Political cartoonists are pre-eminent
image makers and breakers and, because of that,
they wield real power.' The legendary editor of the
Daily Mirror, Hugh Cudlipp, was of a similar
opinion. He thought that Philip Zec's VE Day
cartoon played a major role in winning Labour the
1945 general election. The image, depicting a
wounded, battle-weary soldier holding the laurels of
peace, was reprinted on the front page of the
Mirror's election issue with the caption, 'Here you
are – don't lose it again!' It served as a blunt
reminder of the promise of David Lloyd George's
Liberal government to build 'a land fit for heroes'
after the First World War: a promise he had not
kept, and, by implication, one that would also be
beyond the Conservatives.

Philip Zec's VE Day cartoon, which Hugh Cudlipp thought
pivotal in Labour's 1945 election victory.

FULL EXPLANATION

David Low's 'Full Explanation' cartoon from 1945, clarifying his notable absence during the election that year.

Lord Beaverbrook, who owned the *Daily Express* and the *Evening Standard*, also believed that cartoons were a powerful weapon at election time. When he employed David Low on the *Standard* in 1927, he became the first newspaper proprietor to give a cartoonist a contract which allowed them complete freedom in the selection and treatment of their subject matter. Up until then, cartoonists had always been expected to support the editorial line of their respective newspaper. Beaverbrook, a Tory peer, generally honoured his agreement with Low, whose own politics were more in line with those on the left. However, at general elections Low's apparent freedom was severely reined in. Although he was normally free to attack the Tory prime minister, Stanley Baldwin (for whom Beaverbrook had nothing but contempt), during the 1929, 1931 and 1935 general elections, several of Low's anti-Conservative cartoons were refused publication. Other cartoons of his were also altered so as to appear as if they were attacking all three main parties rather than just the Tories. During the 1945 election, Low strangely disappeared for two weeks. The *Evening Standard* explained this by telling its readership that Low's health 'had compelled him to take a rest by the sea'. *Daily Express* journalist and later Labour MP, Tom Driberg, was not the only one to think this 'suspicious'. It was remarkable, to say the least. Low was missing the first general election in ten years; one which offered the electorate the chance to decide who would rebuild Britain after the war. Other left-wing cartoonists, including Philip Zec, felt it was an opportunity of a lifetime, and as a result, threw themselves into it.

Even excluding Beaverbrook's occasional editorial interference, the political freedom enjoyed by David Low – and to a lesser extent his successor at the *Evening Standard*, Vicky – is an exception to the rule which continues to persist. As Neil Kinnock put it, 'Whatever their personal political convictions, cartoonists have usually been flag carriers for the preferences and prejudices of the newspapers employing them.' Those who vehemently disagree with their paper's editorial line tend not to last very long.

Regardless of the politics of the paper that employs them, the vast majority of cartoonists today admit to being varying degrees left of centre. Those who actively support the Conservatives are few and far between, but in the past have included such names as Leslie Illingworth, Sidney Strube and, most notably, Michael Cummings. (The latter was once described by his editor at the *Daily Express*, Derek Jameson, as being 'slightly to the right of Attila the Hun'.) As a result, though most contemporary cartoonists would personally favour a Labour government, they generally prefer it from a professional perspective when the Tories are in power. Cartoonists are reactive, not proactive, and as commentators of political events it is naturally easier for them to be against something rather than for it. Otherwise they would risk becoming dull and repetitive propagandists for the cause, as the legendary pocket cartoonist Sir Osbert Lancaster once suggested:

It's okay when you're in opposition. When you have to be for something then they all fall flat on their faces. Even Low – those splendid attacks on Hitler, Mussolini and the Tories – then he occasionally had to do an idealistic picture of happy young workers marching into the dawn – like a soap ad.

Some contemporary cartoonists do still enjoy a similar degree of freedom to that ostensibly given to David Low. The two big guns of current British cartooning, Steve Bell and Peter Brookes, are sufficiently well established to attack whomever they wish. In terms of their personal politics, both claim to have taken a partisan approach towards Labour in the past (although Brookes admits to having had 'one dalliance with the SDP' and didn't vote for Miliband this time round). In spite of this, neither he nor Bell has ever felt any qualms about attacking the Labour leadership – even at election time. Similarly, Christian Adams says that the *Daily Telegraph* enjoys his 'plague on all your houses' approach, despite it being a Conservative paper. Adams describes himself as apolitical – perhaps surprisingly, given his occupation – echoing Sir Osbert Lancaster in his belief that following one political line makes a cartoonist 'boring and repetitive' in what they have to say. Dave Brown is also free to attack whomever he likes, but mainly due to the *Independent* claiming it is, well, independent of any political affiliation. According to Brown: 'I have no intention either to promote or refrain from criticising one party or another.' Even at the *Independent*, though, there are certain restrictions resulting from the need to appear impartial. Peter Schrank found himself in hot water after 'going native' during the 1997 election, as he later recalled:

I got quite excited about Tony Blair and New Labour. I remember waking up on Friday 8 May quite delirious with excitement and lack of sleep. The first rough I submitted to the Independent on Sunday *was deemed 'creepy', i.e. too enthusiastic. After many other futile attempts, Stephen Fay, the then deputy editor suggested I should calm down and consider the possibility that this might not be the best thing that had ever happened. He was right, of course. Of all the politicians I've drawn I think I've disliked Tony Blair the most.*

Most cartoonists generally have to take a pragmatic, politically flexible approach to general elections depending on the party line of the paper they work for. Indeed, many have moved between diametrically opposed newspapers over the course of their careers: Michael Cummings started off at *Tribune* before he went to the *Daily Express*; Bob Moran moved from the *Morning Star* to the *Daily Telegraph*; and Stanley Franklin went from the *Daily Mirror* to the *Sun*. Steve Bright, too, has worked for newspapers on both sides of the political divide, moving from the *Daily Record* to the *Sun*. As with Christian Adams, Bright says he has no problem with changing allegiance according to the paper he works for: 'There's no huge difference really . . . Since I generally loathe all politicians fairly equally as politicians, and love them all fairly equally as cartoon fodder, it's all good for me!'

Those cartoonists who are supportive of their

paper's editorial line naturally relish the opportunity to be partisan. The drawback with this is that it could be argued that they are only preaching to the converted, thereby diminishing any potential influence they might have on the result of an election. Steve Bell's predecessor at the *Guardian*, Les Gibbard, believed this to be true: 'It's easy for us as we identify popular prejudices and push at an open door. Cabinet ministers may read the *Guardian* but not many Tory voters do.' However, today, with the advent of social media, things are very different. Thanks to Twitter, Facebook and political bloggers, cartoons copied and pasted from newspaper websites (generally without copyright approval) are now seen by people of all political persuasions. Christian Adams, for one, told me that he gets comments about his cartoons from those on the left who would never dream of picking up a copy of the *Daily Telegraph*.

Cartoonists thrive during general elections because it is a time when the public tend to focus far more attention on politics than usual. Christian Adams says that it is the theatre of it all that pleases him most: 'It's a time when politicians come out and are prepared to put their heads above the parapet. It's a great opportunity to be really cruel to them.' Peter Schrank concurs, stating that general elections are a 'bit like Punch and Judy on steroids. During an election the sometimes tedious cut and thrust and daily bitchiness

of UK politics can become exciting and relevant.' Similarly, according to Ingram Pinn: 'UK politicians are even more likely to make fools of themselves in the run up to an election, and the usual crass advertising campaigns provide a lot of imagery to mock. MPs actually have to leave their cosy nests in Westminster and meet some of their stroppy constituents for a change, which often leaves them reeling in panic.'

For other cartoonists who are not always overtly political, general elections are an opportunity for them to change tack. MAC, who tends to concentrate on the social and humorous side of British life, finds that at election time his cartoons tend to focus far more on political affairs. Likewise, Ingram Pinn at the *Financial Times* gets more of a chance to turn his attention to the domestic political scene, rather than the international issues he normally concentrates on.

Some cartoonists take the opportunity during an election to be part of the media scrum that closely follows the party leaders around on their campaign tours. Apart from the party conferences, it is a great chance to see up close how the main propagandists behave and react. However, during the 2010 election, Steve Bell got closer than he could ever have imagined. At a motorway service station on the Tory campaign trail, he literally bumped into David Cameron. According to the cartoonist, the Conservative leader confronted him and said:

Steve Bell's iconic depiction of Cameron with a condom over his head.

'The condom, where does that come from?' And I said it was to do with the smoothness of his complexion. He seemed genuinely interested, claiming to have enjoyed the one I'd drawn of him that day as a large sausage on a butcher's weighing machine. I said he wasn't supposed to, and ventured to ask what drugs he was on for this lunatic election marathon. He laughed and said he'd just bought a Patricia Cornwell novel to put himself to sleep on the bus.

Other cartoonists, including Dave Brown, prefer to keep their distance. Brown feels that the drawback of joining the media scrum on the campaign trail or at party conferences is that, although doing so may provide plenty of material, you can risk picking up an idea for your cartoon which the reader is unlikely to comprehend. The general public are at best likely to see just a few seconds of actual coverage, and so may fail to pick up on references to a particular story.

The 2015 general election proved a difficult one for the cartoonists, as the pollsters got it badly wrong, as they also did in 1992. For weeks, influenced by the apparent dead heat in the polls between Labour and the Conservatives, cartoonists drew images depicting a hung parliament after the election. Bob Moran, for one, believed the pollsters' predictions gave him limited options: 'I had been looking forward to the election as it was to be my first since becoming a cartoonist. However, a boring campaign and a seemingly predictable outcome made the whole thing feel quite disappointing.' Fortunately for Moran, the exit polls on election day changed all that: 'Everything changed when the shock result was announced. All the roughed-out ideas based on coalition talks were screwed up, along with the careers of many of the people I'd been drawing for the last five years. So, in the end, it turned out to be a very exciting election to cover.'

As Moran's comments confirm, the most testing

Les Gibbard's ill-fated attempt to predict the outcome of the 1970 general election, before and after.

cartoon to draw during an election is actually the one drawn on polling day for the next day's newspaper. Having to predict a scenario for the following morning can be full of pitfalls at the best of times. Peter Brookes states you cannot afford to 'take a punt' in case you get it badly wrong and end up with egg on your face. So it came as no surprise in this year's election that, in the cartoons published the day after the Conservatives had gained a surprise majority in the House of Commons, Britain's political cartoonists had shied away from attempting to predict the result.

In the past, some cartoonists have been brave or foolish enough to risk trying to hedge their bets on the final outcome of the ballot. On the day of the June 1970 general election, Les Gibbard, believing the polls were right to suggest that Labour would win, 'took a punt' and drew a cartoon of Harold Wilson as a jack-in-the-(ballot)-box. When it became

clear that Edward Heath had won a surprise victory, Gibbard was forced to make a quick change to the first cartoon, superimposing Edward Heath's head on top of Wilson's.

If the election seems to be a tight one, as we have just seen this past year, cartoonists, as I have said, play it safe. At the 2010 election, this approach paid dividends for Andy Davey in the *Sun*, as he later recalled:

I had drawn a non-committal cartoon for the Sun *since we didn't know what the election result was going to be. So I drew the party leaders all exhausted after having beaten each other up in a polling station fight. As they lie there with black eyes, they all share the same thought bubble: 'Now what?' Nobody knew what to expect and the result was not clear even by Friday morning, so, luckily for me, it turned out to be pretty correct. Paddy Ashdown went on the* Today *programme and said: 'I don't normally advocate anyone to do this but I urge all readers to go out, buy themselves a copy of the* Sun *and turn to the cartoon on page 8 which summarises the situation perfectly.' This was against the grain because of his chequered history with the paper ('Paddy Pantsdown', etc.). Thank you, Paddy.*

These days, political parties try their best to manage their parliamentary candidates during election campaigns, warning them not to say or do anything untoward which might in any way lessen their chances of winning. Cartoonists find this increasingly frustrating. Candidates who watch their every word and are unable to speak their minds freely can make commentating on elections not only difficult, but increasingly dull and tedious, too. According to Scott Clissold:

> *Everything is so stage-managed and controlled now during campaigns that it can be a godsend when something interesting happens. Even if it's John Prescott punching the protester or the Gordon Brown and Mrs Duffy 'bigot' incident. Most campaigns are pretty boring, though, which is probably how the politicians prefer them.*

Andy Davey's polling station punch-up from the 2010 election.

In comparison to previous campaigns, Peter Brookes at first found the last election boring primarily because the candidates were 'on message and only invited supporters were allowed at leaders' events'. He described it as 'easily the dullest (so far) that I've worked through, and I just wish something would HAPPEN. Somehow, the fuss generated by that idiot [Michael] Fallon isn't quite enough'. Brookes did, however, find the election 'much better later on, and of course the night itself was anything but boring'. Dave Brown thinks another reason elections have become duller is due to the fact that parties now rely less on advertising billboards to get their message across. In the past, they could be seen all over the country plastered with party propaganda. 'They were great fun to parody,' he says. Now, you get the odd mobile van advert, but the imagery is not around long enough to become embedded in the public's consciousness.

This does not mean, however, that today's political cartoonists yearn for a time prior to the introduction of fixed-term parliaments in 2011, when prime ministers could call an early election if they thought there was a good chance of winning. According to Martin Rowson, this too had a tendency to result in predictable, unexciting elections:

In the past it's been mainly boring. 1987 foregone; 1992 depressing; 1997 foregone but exhilarating (fresh meat); 2001 boring; 2005 boring and depressing; 2010 foregone but embarrassing, with a nice surprise at the end. I liked 2010 because it gave me an opportunity to engage in a step change with the creation of Clegnocchio. At a deeper level, I think I can date my current feeling of furious ennui to last May, when we should have had an election: every parliament since 1979 has been four years, except Major and Brown, which dragged on because they knew they'd lose, so the final year was excitingly grim and slapstick chaotic. This time, my inner satirist has been yearning for nine months for fresh meat (which every new government is, even if same party), hence my fury at how boring it all is.

Martin's wish for 'fresh meat' after an election resonates with many cartoonists. It offers them the refreshing challenge of working on new faces and characters thrown up either by a new incoming government or changes within an existing cabinet. Many tire of having to continue drawing the same old faces year after year. Ingram Pinn thinks 'there is pleasure in seeing some of them booted out by the voters'. For Steve Bell, the 2015 election result was a double whammy. Not only did Labour lose badly, but he has to continue depicting David Cameron as Prime Minister, which appears to irk him. According to Bell: 'The election was a disaster. Now we've got Cameron for another five years. I'm so fed up with drawing that c**t!'

Of course it can also work the other way, as Scott Clissold explains: 'It might be the last time you get to draw a bunch of politicians you really love drawing or have only just got a good handle on capturing.' After the last election, Peter Brookes had mixed feelings about losing his most successful cartoon creation so far, when Shadow Chancellor Ed Balls lost his seat and Ed Miliband resigned as Labour leader. His depiction of them as Wallace and Gromit had been hugely successful, frequently mentioned in the House of Commons as well as receiving widespread coverage in the media. Brookes did say that despite losing Miliband and

Balls, there had been limitations to what he could do with them as Wallace and Gromit without besmirching what, in essence, is a children's favourite. Most cartoonists were sad to see Ed Miliband go as he offered them such wonderful material with those big panda eyes and teeth that went on for ever. However, the bacon sandwich and the 'Ed Stone' moments were themselves beyond parody. According to Bob Moran, 'It's nice to have some new faces to draw but Ed Miliband had been my favourite subject and, from that point of view alone, I was sorry to see the back of him.' In comparison, no one was sad to see Nick Clegg resign as Lib Dem leader after his party's disastrous showing at the election. Despite the fact that, as Dave Brown has said, 'everyone had developed their own version of Nick Clegg,' it had been a constant struggle for cartoonists to get a good likeness of him. This most put down to the apparent blandness of his facial features.

So, do political cartoonists really make a

The last we will see of Peter Brookes's depiction of the two Eds as Wallace and Gromit?

difference at election time? The answer is probably not. What they certainly can do is to entertain us by visually illuminating the major election issues and incidents. They also add colour, vitriol and great humour to the proceedings. Without them, general elections would simply be far less fun and, undeniably, far less interesting.

THE CARTOONS

10 August 2014
Chris Riddell
Observer

Boris Johnson put an end to speculation by announcing his intention to return to Parliament at the next election. This was widely seen as a staging post in a campaign to replace David Cameron. Johnson's aspirations for becoming a future prime minister were given a boost by an opinion poll which suggested that support for the Tories would increase by 6% if he were to replace Cameron as leader.

Islamic State militants killed at least 500 members of Iraq's Yazidi minority, burying some alive and taking hundreds of women as slaves. The Yazidis, followers of an ancient religion derived from Zoroastrianism, are branded as 'devil worshippers' by ISIS insurgents, who have ordered them to convert to Islam or die.

16 August 2014
Morten Morland
The Times

According to the cartoonist: 'During the obsession with the "Ice Bucket Challenge", we saw many notable figures throwing buckets of icy water over their heads. This included ex-president George Dubya Bush, who posted a rather sickly video of himself partaking in this altruistic fad. This may have been for charity but nonetheless I couldn't help but make the link between this and the use of the "waterboarding" torture technique used by the US during Bush's war on terror.'

22 August 2014
Ben Jennings
Guardian

The threat of ISIS led old enemies into an awkward tangle of new alliances. The US, along with Iran, gave military support to Shiite militia, which had previously battled US forces after the overthrow of Saddam Hussein. Russia supplied military equipment to Iraq, putting it on the same side as the US while confrontation over Ukraine continued. In addition, many Iraqi Shiites and the Lebanese militia Hezbollah, who had gone to Syria to defend the Assad regime, were now fighting ISIS. Saudi Arabia had now also aligned with Iran in its fear that ISIS could destabilise the region, having earlier been accused of being complicit in the ISIS takeover of much of northern Iraq.

23 August 2014
Martin Rowson
Guardian

24 August 2014
Peter Schrank
Independent on Sunday

Three British men believed to be waging jihad alongside ISIS were named in the hunt for the masked extremist who had killed hostage James Foley in a brutal propaganda video. According to the cartoonist: 'James Foley and his fellow captives had nicknamed their captors "the Beatles" because of their British accents. A cruel irony, as they position themselves at the extreme opposite end to any peace and love philosophy. I drew them as buffoons and idiots, which is what they are.'

According to the cartoonist: 'The defection of Tory MP Douglas Carswell to UKIP, coupled with all polls suggesting he was heading for victory as UKIP's first elected MP (and with the likelihood of an increased majority at that), combined as a wake-up call to the Tories that they could no longer claim that nobody was interested in Europe and EU membership.'

1 September 2014
Steve Bright
Sun

On 30 August, the Israeli government announced the expropriation of an estimated 988 acres of Palestinian land belonging to five villages situated south of Bethlehem. The cabinet stated that the land had been taken in response to the kidnapping and killing of three Israeli youths by Hamas militants, which had taken place in the same area in June. Meanwhile in Yalta, President Vladimir Putin described the annexation (or 'reunification') of the Crimea as 'therapy' for a deep trauma; 'a wound inflicted on our people as the result of the dramatic schism of the 20th century'.

2 September 2014
Steve Bell
Guardian

TOUGHER MEASURES FOR RETURNING JIHADISTS...

PASSPORT CONTROL

David Cameron announced tougher measures against Britons planning to fight with extremists in Iraq and Syria, and those wishing to return to launch attacks on home soil. Cameron also stated that his government would enhance police powers to temporarily strip departing suspects of passports at the border. According to the cartoonist: 'This is the kind of "real life" experience I would love David Cameron to have. Talk about getting your hands dirty.'

2 September 2014
Brian Adcock
Independent

7 September 2014
Chris Riddell
Observer

In response to the growing crisis in Ukraine, NATO decided to form a 4,000-strong 'spearhead' force capable of being deployed anywhere in the world within 48 hours. The force was part of a number of measures taken by NATO in response to the annexation of Crimea by Russia and the increasingly violent civil war being fought in the east of the country by separatist forces with Russian backing.

The Rev. Ian Paisley, former Democratic Unionist Party leader and first minister of Northern Ireland, died on 12 September, aged 88. Mr Paisley, a Protestant preacher, was the face of hard-line unionism throughout the Troubles, famed as much for his thunderous speeches as for his uncompromising political stance.

13 September 2014
Martin Rowson
Guardian

According to the cartoonist: 'The Scottish independence referendum outcome became too close to call. The Better Together camp seemed panic-stricken during the final few weeks. Alex Salmond and the Yes camp had chipped away at their lead and an independent Scotland appeared a real possibility with less than a week to go. There was a feeling that the Union was about to unravel.'

14 September 2014
Scott Clissold
Sunday Express

The Senate approved President Obama's controversial proposal to arm and train moderate Syrian rebels in an attempt to defeat ISIS. However, there were concerns on both sides of the political divide that weapons given to the rebels could end up in the hands of terrorists. Republican senator Rand Paul described the plan as 'ludicrous', stating: 'No one knows where these arms are going to wind up . . . We don't even know who these groups are.'

18 September 2014
Kevin Kallaugher
The Economist

According to the cartoonist: 'As Scotland moved towards the independence vote, Alex Salmond's bravado did not extend to cutting adrift from the British pound, which he clung to in spite of the fact that an independent Scotland would no longer have the financial backing of the Bank of England. Scottish banks did not share Salmond's optimism as the Royal Bank of Scotland and Lloyds planned to move their holding companies to London to retain Bank of England support.'

18 September 2014
Ingram Pinn
Financial Times

David Cameron faced an angry backlash from Tory backbenchers over last-minute 'bribes' to secure a No vote in Scotland's referendum. Several senior Conservative MPs had become alarmed at the promises of further devolution and more cash for Scotland made by Cameron, Miliband and Clegg. Some even called for Cameron's resignation, denouncing the 'amateur, schoolboy' team responsible for the No campaign, and warning that Cameron could go down in history as 'the prime minister who lost the Union'.

19 September 2014
Christian Adams
Daily Telegraph

20 September 2014
Dave Brown
Independent

According to the cartoonist: 'The cross-party No campaign triumphed in the Scottish referendum and Alex Salmond resigned.'

After the referendum, David Cameron was caught on camera saying that the Queen had 'purred down the line' when he phoned her to say Scotland had voted against independence. Cameron was overheard making the comments to Michael Bloomberg, the former mayor of New York, and later issued a personal apology to the Queen, saying that he was 'very embarrassed' for this extraordinary breach of protocol.

23 September 2014
Paul Thomas
Daily Express

23 September 2014
Peter Brookes
The Times

In his keynote speech to the Labour party conference in Manchester, Ed Balls set out how he planned to 'balance the books' by 2020. He admitted to a long list of 'mistakes' made by the last Labour government, but said the party had learnt from these and would not 'flinch' from making tough decisions if it regained power.

Ed Miliband was criticised for forgetting to mention the country's £75 billion deficit during his speech to the Labour party conference. Speaking without notes, he left out a key section on Labour's plans for tackling the issue. Miliband said: 'I cannot simply memorise a whole speech . . . I could have done it with autocue but I think what people want is somebody who will come and talk to them directly.' George Osborne (who Bell routinely depicts in bondage gear as a reflection of the chancellor's penchant for cuts and restraint) tweeted immediately after the speech to point out Miliband's 'extraordinary' omission.

25 September 2014
Steve Bell
Guardian

According to the cartoonist: 'This cartoon was originally just supposed to be the Tories in their boat on the way to their Birmingham conference. The newspapers were full of pictures of George Clooney in a similar boat at his wedding in Venice. As I was leaving the office, Mark Reckless announced his defection to UKIP so I rushed back and put him on the jet ski using some computer wizardry.'

28 September 2014
Bob Moran
Daily Telegraph

According to the cartoonist: 'George Osborne scrapped the pensions "death tax", finding a £150 million sweetener for the Tory conference, despite the £30 billion cuts still to come.'

30 September 2014
Dave Brown
Independent

'Before I turn round – is that you, Ed?'

2 October 2014
Stan McMurtry
Daily Mail

At the Conservative party conference, David Cameron warned voters that backing UKIP at the next election would only make a Labour government more likely. Cameron's exact words were: 'On 7 May you could go to bed with Nigel Farage, and wake up with Ed Miliband. I don't know about you but not one bit of that works for me.'

In a week to forget for the Conservatives, Brooks Newmark resigned as minister for civil society after sending a graphic photo exposing himself whilst wearing a pair of paisley pyjamas to a journalist posing as a 20-year-old Tory activist. Five days later, David Cameron's attempt to deliver a rousing speech at the Conservative party conference backfired after an unfortunate Freudian slip. Misreading his autocue, the prime minister announced that the Conservative party 'resents' poor children who grow up on housing estates, rather than 'represents'.

2 October 2014
Steve Bell
Guardian

At the Liberal Democrat party conference, Nick Clegg accused his party's coalition partners of 'beating up on the poor', and instructed his leading ministers to 'brutalise' the Tories after George Osborne set out his plans to eliminate the budget deficit by freezing benefits whilst exempting the rich from further tax increases. Clegg told senior Lib Dems to appeal to 'soft Tories' by spreading the message that the chancellor was taking Conservatives back to the era of the nasty party. Meanwhile, a YouGov poll showed increasing support for UKIP from former Lib Dem voters.

6 October 2014
Martin Rowson
Guardian

In response to the electoral threat of UKIP, David Cameron pledged to make migrant reforms a focal point of the forthcoming renegotiation of Britain's relationship with the EU. Jean-Claude Juncker, the incoming president of the European Commission, reacted in no uncertain terms, describing Cameron's proposal to impose limits on the free movement of people within the EU as a 'historic mistake'.

12 October 2014
Chris Riddell
Observer

12 October 2014
Bob Moran
Daily Telegraph

According to the cartoonist: 'This was one of those cartoons where it needed to be more cheeky than actually critical. Most of the press coverage of Boris's Churchill book [published that month] was once again speculating on his own political ambitions. Bearing in mind many *Daily Telegraph* readers are fond of Boris, this seemed like the right sort of image. I think his hand was originally the offensive way round but I was asked to turn it.'

UKIP leader Nigel Farage was invited to take part in a general election TV debate with David Cameron, Ed Miliband and Nick Clegg. The proposals came in for criticism by the SNP, the Green Party and Plaid Cymru, all of which parties were excluded. The most common phrase during the 2010 election debate, used by both Cameron and Brown, was 'I agree with Nick Clegg'.

14 October 2014
Steve Bell
Guardian

16 October 2014
Kevin Kallaugher
The Economist

At the Catholic Church synod, Pope Francis's proposals for wider acceptance of gay people were abandoned. A draft report issued halfway through the meeting, and published in full at the Pope's behest, included a paragraph stating that homosexuals had 'gifts and qualities to offer to the Christian community'. However, the proposals were not approved by the synod, and were consequently deleted from the final text.

South African athlete Oscar Pistorius was given a five-year prison sentence for killing his girlfriend Reeva Steenkamp. He was sent to Pretoria's Kgosi Mampuru II (formerly known as Pretoria Central Prison), where he was housed in a cell in the jail's hospital wing.

22 October 2014
Paul Thomas
Daily Express

An opinion poll suggested that Tory defector Mark Reckless was on course to win back his Commons seat in the Rochester and Strood by-election, in what would be a major victory for UKIP. The week's other main headline was the ongoing supermarket price war between Tesco and discounters such as Aldi and Lidl. According to the cartoonist: 'All cartoonists love joining two stories, but when two images can be joined almost exactly it's Christmas. I was so pleased that Lidl has four letters as does UKIP, but both having an "i" was just perfect. Sounds a small thing, but it really made it complete. (Tesco and Tories both beginning with a "t" was another gift.)'

24 October 2014
Christian Adams
Daily Telegraph

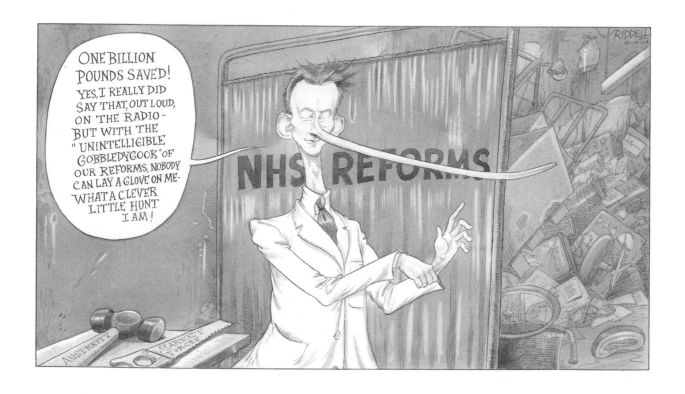

Unnamed sources in Downing Street were quoted as saying that the former health secretary Andrew Lansley's reorganisation of the NHS was the worst mistake of the coalition government, describing his 2012 Health and Social Care Act as 'unintelligible gobbledygook'. Jeremy Hunt attempted to defend his predecessor by claiming that the reforms had cost £1.5 billion to implement but had saved £1 billion a year in NHS administrative costs.

26 October 2014
Chris Riddell
Observer

27 October 2014
Morten Morland
The Times

David Cameron's plans to impose a cap on immigration from the EU were blocked by Angela Merkel. The German chancellor dismissed the prospect of any radical change, saying: 'Germany will not tamper with the fundamental principles of free movement in Europe.'

According to the cartoonist: 'Tony Blair declared Labour unelectable under Ed Miliband, and predicted David Cameron would remain in Downing Street. My cartoon reflects the (mis)fortunes of all party leaders at the time. Blair has reportedly written off Ed's chances of winning the next election because Labour had failed to persuade the country it was fit to govern.'

27 October 2014
Steve Bright
Sun

30 October 2014
Martin Rowson
Guardian

David Cameron was criticised for refusing to be photographed in a pro-feminism T-shirt, when Clegg and Miliband had agreed to do so. The prime minister was repeatedly asked to wear a T-shirt produced by equal rights campaign group the Fawcett Society, with the slogan, 'This is what a feminist looks like.' *Elle*'s editor-in-chief said: 'We asked the prime minister five times if he would wear the T-shirt and send us a snapshot. Five times, he declined . . . It seems the prime minister still has an issue with the word "feminist".'

Maureen Lipman made a personal attack on Ed Miliband after he supported a motion recognising the state of Palestine. Writing on the Commons vote, she said: 'I'm an actress, Ed, and I am often commended for my timing. Frankly, my dear, yours sucks.' The actress announced she would vote for 'almost any other' party until Labour is 'once more led by mensches' – a Yiddish term for a person of integrity and honour.

31 October 2014
Peter Brookes
The Times

Ed Miliband was accused of looking 'awkward' and 'terrified' while photographed giving money to a woman begging on the street. According to the cartoonist: 'This one combined the rising fortunes of Farage, nicking support from all corners of the political spectrum (pardon mixed metaphors), and Miliband's very unfortunate photo opportunity where he awkwardly put 2p into a beggar's cup, unable to look her in the eye, as the cameras snapped.'

1 November 2014
Steve Bright
Sun

'No, not that one ... further over ... left a bit ... I ordered a red one with an extra long stem ...'

Volunteers began removing the ceramic remembrance poppies that made up the *Blood-Swept Lands and Seas of Red* installation at the Tower of London. Each poppy represented the death of a British and Commonwealth soldier during the First World War. All of the poppies that made up the installation were sold off, raising millions of pounds to be shared equally among six service charities.

12 November 2014
Stan McMurtry
Daily Mail

THE RELAUNCH...

14 November 2014
Dave Brown
Independent

According to the cartoonist: 'In a speech signalled as his most important since becoming leader, Ed Miliband attempted to win over voters who doubted he was a credible prime minister.'

OWN GOAL

According to the cartoonist: 'FIFA's astonishing decision to award the 2022 World Cup to Qatar, and allegations of corruption in the bidding process for 2018 (awarded to Russia), prompted FIFA's Sepp Blatter to commission a report by US lawyer Michael Garcia probing the circumstances of the votes for both Qatar and Russia. FIFA suppressed publication of the full report and Hans-Joachim Eckert, chairman of FIFA's ethics committee, claimed any breaches of the regulations had been very limited. FIFA were then plunged into further turmoil by Garcia, who issued a statement saying the summary was incomplete and erroneous. I drew Eckert trying to clear the corruption report ball from FIFA's goal only to have it rebound from Garcia with the increasingly ludicrous Blatter looking on. The case continues.'

15 November 2014
Ingram Pinn
Financial Times

16 November 2014
Dave Simonds
Observer

According to the cartoonist: 'I drew George Osborne and David Cameron as Steph and Dom from Channel 4's popular TV programme *Gogglebox* sneering at Ed Miliband, as they made a good couple to spoof. It particularly seemed to suit Osborne, dressing him up in a pair of high-heeled leather boots.'

According to the cartoonist: 'At the G20 summit in Brisbane, Australia, the Russian leader Vladimir Putin continued to deny he was involved in taking land in the east of Ukraine. Putin left the summit early after speculation that he was being harassed by world leaders over his position on the war in Ukraine. An earlier photo op of the leaders with koalas provided the gag for this cartoon.'

17 November 2014
Brian Adcock
Independent

19 November 2014
Steve Bell
Guardian

Ed Miliband was left looking bewildered during a TV debate after singer Myleene Klass criticised him over his proposed mansion tax policies. As Miliband sought to defend the tax as a means of raising extra funding for the NHS, Klass said the proposed policy would hit 'little grannies' living in modest homes in London rather than the super-rich. As the row continued, viewers took to Twitter, with one writing: 'You know it's gone truly surreal when Myleene Klass goes full Paxman on Miliband.'

Emily Thornberry resigned from Labour's front bench after tweeting a photo during the Rochester and Strood by-election showing a terraced house adorned with three England flags, and with a white van parked outside. Political opponents and some Twitter users accused her of looking down on the occupants of the house. According to the cartoonist: 'UKIP used this cartoon as their Christmas card. But they forgot to ask for permission. Suddenly the digital world went crazy . . . It was definitely cock-up rather than conspiracy. (They ended up paying the copyright fee to the *Daily Telegraph* charity.)'

22 November 2014
Christian Adams
Daily Telegraph

23 November 2014
Chris Riddell
Observer

UKIP called for the children of immigrants to be classed as migrants, seemingly overlooking the fact that Nigel Farage's own two children would be included in that number. Citing a report issued by Migration Watch UK, the party suggested that excluding children born to foreign parents from immigration statistics had led to the overall impact of immigration on population growth being underestimated by more than 1.3 million. Farage himself tweeted that '84% of population growth between 2001 and 2012 was due to migration', if children born in the UK to migrant parents were included in the statistics.

Home Secretary Theresa May unveiled new measures to tackle terrorism, suggesting that the threat faced by the UK was 'perhaps greater than it has ever been'. Campaigners warned that her new counter-terrorism bill could threaten civil liberties, particularly since internet providers would be required to retain Internet Protocol address data 'to identify individual users of internet services'.

24 November 2014
Morten Morland
The Times

In the event of a Labour victory in the general election, Shadow Education Secretary Tristram Hunt said that Britain's private schools would lose £700 million in business rate relief unless they agreed to do more to help improve the quality of education in state schools. Mr Hunt accused the Conservatives of having 'done nothing to breach this Berlin Wall in our education system'.

26 November 2014
Dave Brown
Independent

'I'm sorry her day was ruined...No, I can't do it all again...Please don't swear...Yes, I know who you are...Oh really?...And the same to you Mr Mellor!'

Former Tory cabinet minister David Mellor said he regretted losing his temper after being recorded calling a taxi driver a 'sweaty, stupid little shit' and telling him to 'fuck off'. The argument related to a route Mellor wanted to travel following a visit to Buckingham Palace with his partner, who had just received a CBE. Mellor rebuked the driver for ruining 'a wonderful day' and was heard saying to him: 'You've been driving a cab for ten years, I've been in the cabinet, I'm an award-winning broadcaster, I'm a Queen's Counsel.'

27 November 2014
Stan McMurtry
Daily Mail

On 28 November, David Cameron, in response to growing support for UKIP, delivered a long-awaited speech addressing public concerns on EU migration. According to the cartoonist: 'White van man is a rather lovely stereotype, and a broad, easy target for cartoonists. Especially for one who enjoys drawing cars and vehicles, as I do. And how strange that a party dominated by equally stereotypical toffs should have such appeal to working-class people.'

30 November 2014
Peter Schrank
Independent on Sunday

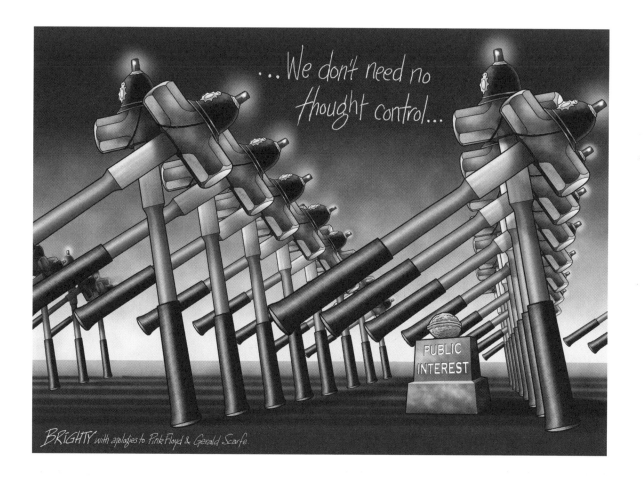

According to the cartoonist: 'The police's heavy-handed actions against journalists arrested, accused and awaiting trial – three years in some cases – for crimes almost all have so far been cleared of. The force of many sledgehammers being used to crack the nut of "public interest". Pink Floyd's classic scene of the marching hammers came to mind, changed to helmeted sledgehammers with flashing blue lights. The "thought control" line fitted perfectly.'

1 December 2014
Steve Bright
Sun

1 December 2014
Gary Barker
The Times

According to the cartoonist: 'The cartoon refers to George Osborne's pledge to give £2 billion extra funding to the NHS, which was facing a winter crisis in A&E especially. This amount was way too little to fix the problems, with health chiefs claiming they would need four times that amount just to tread water.'

Psychos' Greetings

Qu'est-ce que c'est ... fa-fa-fa, fa-la-la-la-lah, la-la-lah-laah!

According to the cartoonist: 'The unnatural pose and rictus grins of Tony and Cherie Blair's Christmas card led some to doubt its authenticity. Meanwhile Gordon Brown announced that he would stand down at the next election, leading to renewed discussion about his relationship with his predecessor.'

3 December 2014
Dave Brown
Independent

5 December 2014
Steve Bell
Guardian

Just minutes before George Osborne delivered his Autumn Statement, David Cameron was left visibly embarrassed after accusing Ed Balls of 'political maso-sadism'. Cameron went on to explain, 'I meant to say masochism,' to which the shadow chancellor responded with an equally cringeworthy 'whip-crack' gesture.

According to the cartoonist: 'Politicians are always complaining of BBC bias when coverage isn't favourable. With just months to go before the general election it was George Osborne's turn. He was furious after a BBC political reporter described the chancellor's plans for spending cuts as "utterly terrifying" with spending being hacked back to 1930s levels. Back to the land of George Orwell's *The Road to Wigan Pier*. Labour were delighted!'

7 December 2014
Scott Clissold
Sunday Express

7 December 2014
Steve Bright
Sun

Nigel Farage backed the decision of Claridge's hotel to ask a breastfeeding woman to cover up, saying that mothers should 'perhaps sit in the corner' when they breastfeed. According to the cartoonist: 'Farage made a statement that women should not breastfeed in public . . . Need I say more?'

In America, a grand jury decided that the white police officer who fatally shot an unarmed black teenager should not be sent to trial. The shooting of 18-year-old Michael Brown in August had led to days of clashes between protesters and police in Ferguson, Missouri and there was further unrest following the grand jury's decision.

8 December 2014
Morten Morland
The Times

According to the cartoonist: 'Wee Eck, as he is known in Scotland, is always good value for the political cartoonist. If he is successful in running for the Lib Dem-held seat of Gordon he will no doubt ruffle a few feathers when he returns to Westminster. Salmond has said the 2015 election could put his party in a commanding position. I'm looking forward to it.'

8 December 2014
Brian Adcock
Independent

According to the cartoonist: 'This was interesting for me because, being a relatively young cartoonist, I'd never had any cause to cover the Northern Ireland peace process. I think there was some debate as to whether it was too early for a full-blown Christmas theme but fortunately it worked because the story was about Cameron missing his Christmas Eve deadline for a new agreement on questions such as welfare reform and dealing with the legacy of the Troubles.'

13 December 2014
Bob Moran
Daily Telegraph

14 December 2014
Scott Clissold
Sunday Express

According to the cartoonist: 'David Miliband hinted about a possible return to Westminster. Brother Ed was already under pressure from his own party and with the general election looming it probably wasn't the early Christmas present Ed was hoping for.'

BRAVEARSE ...

According to the cartoonist: 'William Hague attempted to introduce "English votes for English laws", a plan hastily announced by David Cameron after the Scottish referendum.'

17 December 2014
Dave Brown
Independent

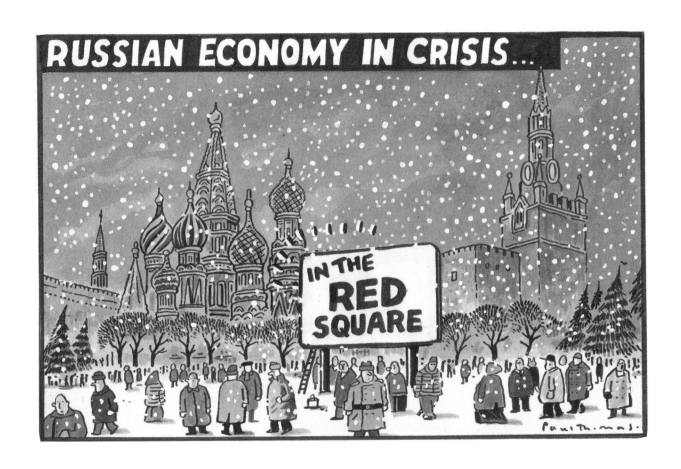

The Russian economy contracted for the first time in five years, leaving the country on the verge of recession due to falling oil prices and Western sanctions over its role in the Ukraine crisis. However, Vladimir Putin denied pursuing an 'aggressive' foreign policy, stating that Russia was not 'encroaching on anyone's interests – just protecting our own'. The president insisted that the dramatic fall in the rouble would be reversed, blaming 'outside factors' for the currency hitting an all-time low of 80 per US dollar.

19 December 2014
Paul Thomas
Daily Express

According to the cartoonist: 'This cartoon was on the controversial release of a comedy about two journalists instructed to assassinate Kim Jong-un [*The Interview*]. North Korea supposedly threatened a merciless retaliation against the US if this film were to be released. Here we have the rather small Supreme Leader casting a large shadow over the Hollywood hills.'

20 December 2014
Ben Jennings
i

BREAKING THE ICE

According to the cartoonist: 'Barack Obama announced the tentative restoration of diplomatic relations with Cuba after more than five decades of hostility. The sanctions began in 1960 at the time of the cold war and were extended in 1962 after the Cuban missile crisis. Neither country has benefitted from the sanctions and the Cuban economy has been hit very hard, especially when they lost Russian support after the dissolution of the USSR. More recently Obama has met the Cuban president Raul Castro and apologised to him, although sanctions are still in place.'

20 December 2014
Ingram Pinn
Financial Times

According to the cartoonist: 'This cartoon was on the subject of anti-austerity sentiment in Greece leading to the upsurge in support for the left-wing party Syriza, which ended up gaining power in early 2015. During the eurozone crises, violent clashes between anti-austerity protesters and riot police were a memorable image. This cartoon shows that this time around those who opposed austerity were using the ballot box to revolt against the status quo.'

31 December 2014
Ben Jennings
Guardian

According to the cartoonist: 'I don't think I've ever been confronted with anything like the murders at *Charlie Hebdo* – people being killed for doing exactly the job that I do. I wanted my response to be true to the spirit of *Charlie Hebdo*. I knew they'd want the magazine to carry on, so it had to be a gesture of defiance. Hence the hand rising out of the newspaper. Drawing it was quite an emotional experience. What drives you as a cartoonist is being angry at things you see as ridiculous, wrong-headed, venal, evil. Compared to the quite realistically drawn newspaper, I tried to make the hand as cartoony as possible. The yellow colouration of the hand is a reference to the work of *Charlie*'s editor-in-chief Stéphane Charbonnier, whose figures were always yellow.'

8 January 2015
Dave Brown
Independent

According to the cartoonist: 'I wonder if David Cameron now regrets his reluctance to debate with Ed Miliband on TV. I think it must have damaged him more than Ed could have done in any TV dust-up. Ed later used the same gag as I have done here in a speech in Edinburgh, saying: "Now we know why the chicken crossed the road – to avoid the TV election debates." Did he pinch it from this cartoon? I like to think so.'

12 January 2015
Brian Adcock
Independent

12 January 2015
Martin Rowson
Guardian

After the series of terrorist attacks in Paris between 7 and 9 January, more than 40 world leaders joined the start of a 'unity' march in the French capital, linking arms in an act of solidarity. Up to 1.6 million people of all ages, religions and nationalities took to the streets not only to show their respect for the victims but also their support for the values of the Republic: 'liberté, égalité, fraternité'.

'Forget Dennis the Menace. Guess what's going on our front page this week ...'

The planned print run of the first *Charlie Hebdo* magazine since the terror attacks was increased to five million after the first run of 60,000 copies sold out within hours of its going on sale. The cover of the 'survivors' issue', as the magazine referred to it, showed a cartoon of the prophet Muhammad weeping whilst holding a sign saying 'Je suis Charlie', with the headline 'Tout est pardonné' ('All is forgiven').

15 January 2015
Stan McMurtry
Daily Mail

16 January 2015
Christian Adams
Daily Telegraph

David Cameron paid a two-day visit to Washington just months before the British general election. Being seen with President Obama was considered a huge boost to Cameron's chances of winning a second term as prime minister. Meanwhile, two climbers had just reached the summit of El Capitan in Yosemite National Park, California. They were the first to do so without aids, except for harnesses and ropes to prevent deadly falls.

At the Golden Globe Awards in Hollywood several stars showed their support for the victims of the terrorist attacks in Paris. According to the cartoonist: 'When Helen Mirren and George Clooney were proclaiming "Je suis Charlie" at the Golden Globe Awards, I started to feel a little queasy . . .'

18 January 2015
Peter Schrank
Independent on Sunday

19 January 2015
Steve Bright
Sun

According to the cartoonist: 'After the *Charlie Hebdo* attack, the Pope suggested that while freedom of speech is great, there are occasions you might well expect a punch for exercising it. Voltaire ("I disapprove of what you say, but I will defend to the death . . ." etc.) being his natural boxing ring opponent on this one.'

Nick Clegg called for a fundamental overhaul of how the NHS deals with the issue of suicide. The deputy prime minister urged hospitals to aim to end all such deaths, saying: 'Suicide is preventable, it is not inevitable.' Elsewhere in the news, the Green Party had taken a small lead over the Liberal Democrats in a new opinion poll.

19 January 2015
Morten Morland
The Times

The cartoon depicts a letter and an illustration:

Department for Communities and Local Government

Leading Fat Bloke
Fat Blokes of Great Britain
Lardcastle
E8E E88

Wibbly Wobbly

We have recently seen terrible atrocities committed by a tiny number (80) of Extremist Fat Blokes who have gobbled up half the entire wealth of the world on their own behalf. The hijacking of a great condition to justify such heinous crimes sickens us all. As Fat Blokes around the world have made clear, such actions are an affront to Fat Blokery. Fat Blokes from across the country have spoken out to say: not in our name.

You, as Fat Bloke Leaders have a precious opportunity and an important responsibility: in explaining and demonstrating how Fat in Blokes can be part of British Identity.

The Rt Hon Eric Pickles MP
Secretary of State

Lord Tariq Ahmad of Wimbledon
Parliamentary Under Secretary of State

Department for Communities and Local Government
Fry Building
Marsham Street
London
SW1P 4DF

Three ways you can help:

1) Email us about the work you are doing to promote the positive image of British Fat Blokes

2) Report Anti-Fat Bloke Hatred To the police online at www.report-it.org.uk

3) Lose weight.

LARD — NOT IN MY NAME

belltoons.co.uk —

©Steve Bell 2015 - 3770.201

20 January 2015
Steve Bell
Guardian

David Cameron defended a letter urging senior Muslim leaders to do more to tackle extremism after the terrorist attacks in Paris. The Muslim Council of Britain criticised the message, written by Communities Secretary Eric Pickles, objecting in particular to 'the implication that extremism takes place at mosques'. Cameron described the letter as 'reasonable, sensible and moderate'.

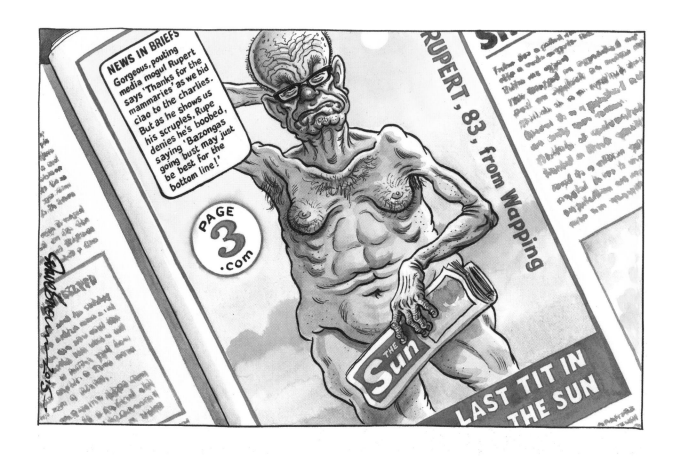

The *Sun* printed a topless model on Page 3 after three days of growing speculation that the controversial feature had been dropped. Topless models were first introduced by the newspaper in 1970, just a year after Rupert Murdoch bought the title.

21 January 2015
Dave Brown
The Times

According to the cartoonist: 'This cartoon came after a week of farcical controversies involving many people associated with UKIP (not a rare occurrence). The party had also just been described by one of its defectors as a "vanity project" for Nigel Farage. I decided to try and depict the UKIP operation based inside the head of their supreme leader, with various clowns working in different departments. I referenced the infographics of Fritz Kahn for this image.'

25 January 2015
Ben Jennings
Guardian

According to the cartoonist: 'The Labour rose was wilting in Scotland as support continued to slide. Every new poll seemed to be worse than the previous one for Ed Miliband, with Labour now fearing a possible SNP landslide at the election.'

25 January 2015
Scott Clissold
Sunday Express
(Scottish Edition)

26 January 2015
Morten Morland
The Times

The anti-austerity party, Syriza, won the general election in Greece, falling just two seats short of an absolute majority. The party leader Alexis Tsipras agreed to form a coalition with the right-wing Independent Greeks party, so becoming prime minister of the first eurozone government openly opposed to bailout conditions imposed by the European Union and International Monetary Fund.

The 50th anniversary of Sir Winston Churchill's funeral was commemorated by a day of events in London. The same boat that carried the former prime minister's coffin along the Thames in 1965 repeated the journey, with members of his family among those on board. David Cameron paid tribute to his predecessor, saying: 'If there is one aspect of this man I admire more than any other, it is Churchill the patriot.' When Churchill made his final journey down the Thames, the cranes on the docks were said to have bowed in honour. In Rowson's cartoon, the docks are long gone, to be replaced by foreign-owned corporate monoliths. 'O tempora, o mores' is a sentence by Cicero which roughly translates as, 'Alas the times, and the manners.'

31 January 2015
Martin Rowson
Guardian

It emerged that Peter Mandelson and Alastair Campbell had approached Alan Johnson to ask whether he would consider taking over from Ed Miliband. The same week, Andy Murray's fiancée Kim Sears had turned up at the men's Australian Open final wearing a black T-shirt with a 'Parental Advisory: Explicit Content' logo on it. The shirt was a response to the controversy she had caused a few days earlier after being seen to mouth, 'Fucking have that, you Czech flash fuck' towards her fiancé's semi-final opponent, Tomas Berdych.

2 February 2015
Morten Morland
The Times

After failing to remember the name of one of Labour's key business supporters, Ed Balls said: 'It's an age thing.' In an interview with BBC *Newsnight*, he described Bill Thomas, the chair of Labour's small business taskforce, simply as 'Bill', and when pressed could not give his surname. David Cameron seized on the gaffe, suggesting that it was evidence that Labour was 'anti-business and anti-enterprise'.

5 February 2015
Peter Brookes
The Times

6 February 2015
Dave Brown
Independent

According to the cartoonist: 'President Hollande and Chancellor Merkel mounted a surprise (though seemingly doomed) peace mission to Kiev, amid increased talk of the West arming Ukraine.'

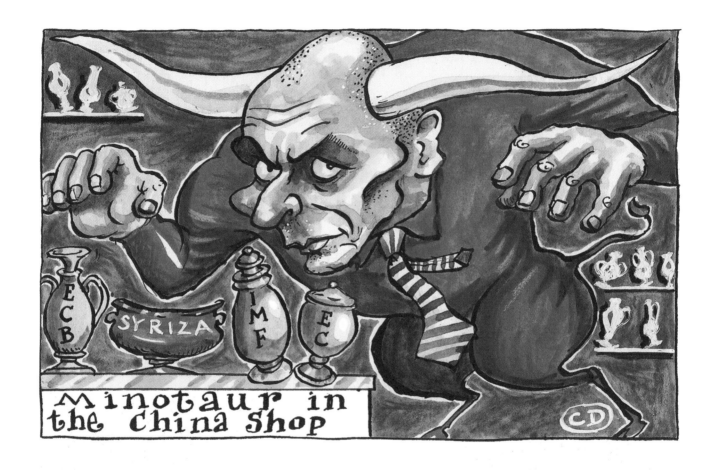

Minotaur in the china shop

According to the cartoonist: 'Greece's new finance minister, Yanis Varoufakis, a self-proclaimed libertarian Marxist, lived up to his billing as the bad boy of global economics. The only thing he didn't do was trash his hotel room. I Hellenised the old bull in the china shop to illustrate his methods, which were in danger of damaging his party Syriza as much as the ECB, IMF or the EC in general. I probably made a mistake in his patriotic tie as I don't think I've ever seen him wear one. Bad boys don't, I'm told.'

7 February 2015
Chris Duggan
The Times

The Plumb pudding in danger

9 February 2015
Morten Morland
The Times

Angela Merkel held talks with Vladimir Putin to try to end the conflict in Ukraine. Speaking at the Munich Security Conference, Merkel warned against provoking Putin, saying: 'I am firmly convinced this conflict cannot be solved with military means.' Morland's cartoon on the matter is a homage to James Gillray's famous print, 'The plumb-pudding in danger', depicting Napoleon and William Pitt carving up the world over a dinner table.

According to the cartoonist: 'The prime minister was in trouble for being overly optimistic. I assumed all *Daily Telegraph* readers would know Vicky's original sarcastic SuperMac cartoon of Harold Macmillan. However, I did get some complaints from left-wing followers on Twitter, saying: "Of all the days, why portray Cameron as Superman today!?"'

11 February 2015
Christian Adams
Daily Telegraph

12 February 2015
Martin Rowson
Guardian

David Cameron was overheard complaining that Ed Miliband was 'personally horrid' to him during a particularly heated Prime Minister's Question Time. Miliband accused Cameron of being 'a dodgy prime minister', saying: 'There is something rotten at the heart of the Tory party and it's you.' Cameron's complaint was overheard as he left the chamber, when he was also heard to say to Conservative ministers that the Labour leader had only hit out 'because he was losing'.

Lord Green of Hurstpierpoint, a former chairman and chief executive of HSBC, was put under pressure by Shadow Treasury Minister Shabana Mahmood with regard to how much he knew about allegations of malpractice during his tenure at the bank. A leaked report had alleged that during Lord Green's time as chief executive, HSBC's Swiss arm had helped 8,844 wealthy Britons avoid millions of pounds in tax. After retiring from HSBC, Lord Green was a Conservative trade and investment minister from 2011 until 2013.

15 February 2015
Chris Riddell
Observer

16 February 2015
Christian Adams
Daily Telegraph

Ed Miliband was accused of hypocrisy after it was claimed that Sir David Garrard, a property tycoon and Labour donor, had placed shares in an offshore trust that could be used to avoid tax. The allegations came shortly after Miliband had claimed that Lord Fink, former treasurer of the Conservative party and a prominent donor, had sought to avoid UK tax.

According to the cartoonist: 'In Denmark's capital, Copenhagen, at an event called "Art, Blasphemy and Freedom of Expression", Omar El-Hussein killed one civilian and wounded three police officers. Swedish artist Lars Vilks was among the speakers and is thought to have been the main target because of his drawings of Muhammad. In an apparent act of anti-Semitism El-Hussein then went on to kill a Jewish man and also wounded two more police officers. El-Hussein was later shot dead by police. After I did this cartoon for the *Independent* a letter appeared in the paper later that week saying: "I cannot remember being moved to tears by a cartoon; Brian Adcock's comment on the Copenhagen attack did it today." That was the best compliment I have ever had.'

16 February 2015
Brian Adcock
Independent

Since Greece's Syriza party came to power, its anti-austerity stance had put it on a collision course with the country's creditors, especially Germany, which contributed the lion's share of the bailouts given to Greece in an attempt to keep the single currency together. According to the cartoonist: 'I always welcome the chance to draw a cartoon about Greece's troubles. I know the country well; I love it and am exasperated by it in equal measure. Yanis Varoufakis is the sort of man we cartoonists love to draw, with a very distinctive face, style and manner.'

18 February 2015
Peter Schrank
Independent

GREETINGS FROM CORNWALL

According to the cartoonist: 'This cartoon was produced after there was a clash in the skies between the RAF and Russian jets over Cornwall. I decided to do a spoof seaside postcard to juxtapose the serene Cornish surroundings with this ominous military tension in the sky.'

21 February 2015
Ben Jennings

i

22 February 2015
Scott Clissold
Sunday Express

Vladimir Putin denied Ukrainian claims that Russian troops were fighting in Crimea. According to the cartoonist: 'Oscar weekend 2015 and Vladimir Putin's aggressive foreign policy was in the news. Where will Vlad the invader be rolling out his red carpet next?'

'Oy! Get off our patch'

The former foreign secretaries Jack Straw and Sir Malcolm Rifkind denied breaking any rules after being secretly filmed offering their services to a private company for cash. An investigation by the *Daily Telegraph* and Channel 4's *Dispatches* alleged that Straw and Rifkind had offered to use their positions as politicians on behalf of a fictitious Chinese company in return for thousands of pounds.

24 February 2015
Stan McMurtry
Daily Mail

According to the cartoonist: 'This cartoon was on the news that, due to the extreme heat in the summer, the 2022 World Cup in Qatar would be held in November. It compares this consideration for the football players' well-being to the awful conditions faced by migrant labourers building the stadiums so that Qatar could be ready to host the World Cup. Many of the workers "belong" to their employer till the job is complete and have to work in temperatures of up to 50°C for a pittance.'

25 February 2015
Ben Jennings
Guardian

As US Secretary of State John Kerry and his Iranian counterpart were negotiating Iran's nuclear future in Geneva, Israeli Prime Minister Benjamin Netanyahu accused America of 'giving up' on trying to stop Iran obtaining nuclear weapons. Kerry questioned Netanyahu's stance on Iran's nuclear programme, stating that the Israeli PM 'may not be correct'.

27 February 2015
Kevin Kallaugher
The Economist

8 March 2015
Dave Simonds
Observer

According to the cartoonist: 'Around this time David Cameron was doing everything he could to get out of appearing in any of the election TV debates, making a long list of demands to be met before he would deign to make an appearance in them. I thought he could be a not very convincing TV "repair" man fixing things with a 50lb mallet.'

David Cameron defended Jeremy Clarkson after the *Top Gear* presenter was suspended for punching a producer in a dispute over catering. Cameron said: 'I don't know exactly what happened. He is a constituent of mine, he is a friend of mine, he is a huge talent . . . Because he is a talent and he does amuse and entertain so many people, including my children who'll be heartbroken if *Top Gear* is taken off air, I hope this can be sorted out, because it is a great programme and he is a great talent.'

11 March 2015
Steve Bell
Guardian

11 March 2015
Dave Brown
Independent

According to the cartoonist: 'Foreign Secretary Philip Hammond attacked "apologists" for terrorism, after advocacy group Cage criticised the security services' role in radicalising "Jihadi John".'

Nigel Farage was criticised for his call to scrap anti-race-discrimination legislation to allow employers to discriminate in favour of British workers. His comments were roundly condemned by politicians and unions who variously described the UKIP leader's proposals as 'shocking', 'divisive and dangerous' and 'deeply concerning'. Shadow Justice Secretary Sadiq Khan accused Farage of 'breathtaking ignorance', saying: 'When my parents moved to London they frequently saw signs saying "no blacks, no dogs, no Irish". What UKIP is suggesting would take us back to those days.'

13 March 2015
Steve Bell
Guardian

14 March 2015
Peter Brookes
The Times

Ed Miliband faced criticism after a video depicting the Labour leader and his wife in the kitchen of their North London home was revealed to have been filmed in their second, smaller kitchen so they would appear more down to earth. The revelation led to some commentators mockingly calling him Ed 'Two Kitchens' Miliband, following in the footsteps of John 'Two Jags' Prescott. Miliband had also been ridiculed earlier in his election campaign after less than flattering pictures had emerged of him trying to eat a bacon sandwich.

According to the cartoonist: 'Although Labour had some good economic policies, they were not getting them across to the electorate. Ed Balls made a speech, made leaden by statistics, which once again failed to make an impact. I recalled the late comedian Frank Carson's catchphrase on *The Comedians*: "It's the way I tell 'em!" The wrecking ball was an allusion to Ball's use of it ending in only hitting himself. As an afterthought I wished I'd just done him as Miley Cyrus to please the youth, though the image would have been quite disturbing.'

14 March 2015
Chris Duggan
The Times

16 March 2015
Brian Adcock
Independent

According to the cartoonist: 'As a partner in the governing coalition the Liberal Democrats' credibility had taken a battering, but despite this Nick Clegg promised that the Lib Dems would be "sticking around" – and they probably will be, much like an annoying bit of chewing gum on the sole of your shoe.'

Tony Blair announced that he would be stepping down from his role as a peace envoy for the Middle East. According to the cartoonist: 'Apparently one insider in the Middle East peace process called Tony Blair an "embarrassment". However, as he leaves his post, that's not going to stop the ever immodest Tone. I love drawing rust – it's easy to do but has a great effect.'

17 March 2015
Christian Adams
Daily Telegraph

'However, this sure beats being in Alex Salmond's pocket, Nicola.'

17 March 2015
Stan McMurtry
Daily Mail

The Conservatives launched a new campaign poster depicting Ed Miliband in Alex Salmond's pocket, reflecting David Cameron's concerns over the SNP being Miliband's 'only route into Number 10'. Scotland's first minister Nicola Sturgeon later suggested that the SNP could enter a deal with Miliband in the event of a hung parliament. However, after the release of the poster Shadow Chancellor Ed Balls said a coalition with the SNP after the 7 May general election was 'not part of Labour's plans'.

According to the cartoonist: 'All budgets are about electioneering, but this year's was so much more than any other. Osborne is definitely canvassing for votes for the general election – and maybe too for a leadership challenge? The simpler the image the better, I always think, and hopefully the little box summed it all up.'

18 March 2015
Christian Adams
Daily Telegraph

23 March 2015
Chris Riddell
Observer

George Osborne came under pressure to spell out details of the £12 billion in welfare cuts needed to avoid further reductions to public services. The chancellor rejected the Office for Budget Responsibility's warning that public spending faced a 'rollercoaster' ride with deeper cuts followed by sharp funding increases, insisting that the watchdog had not taken into account planned economies in welfare and £5 billion of anti-tax-avoidance measures, but refusing to elaborate on exactly where those welfare savings would come from.

Speaking from the kitchen of his Cotswolds home, David Cameron stated: 'I've said I'll stand for a full second term, but I think after that it will be time for new leadership. Terms are like Shredded Wheat: two are wonderful but three might just be too many.' He also took the unusual step of naming his likely successor in 2020 as George Osborne, Theresa May or Boris Johnson. Opponents accused Cameron of taking a third Conservative term for granted, describing his remarks as 'typically arrogant' and 'incredibly presumptuous'.

25 March 2015
Steve Bell
Guardian

27 March 2015
Dave Brown
Independent

According to the cartoonist: 'As Richard III was re-buried in Leicester, Princes Charles failed in a bid to keep his "black spider" letters to ministers secret. The Supreme Court ruled they must be published within weeks.'

According to the cartoonist: 'MPs' expenses would henceforth be known as "operating costs" under a reform supported by Speaker Bercow and approved by parliamentary watchdogs. Lib Dem MP Sir Bob Russell said it was time to do away with the word "expenses" as it implied "something going into an MP's back pocket". Shurely shome mishtake? Meanwhile, 46 MPs were found claiming expenses for London homes even though they already own a property in the capital.'

29 March 2015
Andy Davey
Sun on Sunday

THEY'RE OFF...

David Cameron and Ed Miliband were grilled by Jeremy Paxman in leaders' interviews that fell short of the full-blown debate many had hoped for. According to the cartoonist: 'The starting gun cliché is often used at the beginnings of elections, and can seem rather tired, unless given a fresh twist. After watching Jeremy Paxman cutting politicians down to size over many years on *Newsnight*, I thought it'd be fun to give him the same treatment. Somehow it didn't work out that way. He still seems rather cool and poised, dominating the scene.'

29 March 2015
Peter Schrank
Independent on Sunday

According to a survey, although opinion polls suggested that a hung parliament was increasingly likely to be the result of the upcoming election, five years of coalition had left a significant majority of Britons wanting a return to one-party government. Just 29% of people wanted another coalition in contrast to 62% who would prefer a single party to govern. When the same survey was conducted in 2007, 45% of people had been in favour of a coalition.

30 March 2015
Martin Rowson
Guardian

David Cameron went to Buckingham Palace to inform the Queen of the dissolution of Parliament, starting what he described as 'the most important general election in a generation' – overlooking the fact that the Fixed Term Parliaments Act meant his visit was purely ceremonial. Earlier in the week, Ed Miliband had been bullish during a live TV interview when asked by Jeremy Paxman whether he had got what it took to be a world leader. 'Hell yes, I'm tough enough' was Miliband's response.

30 March 2015
Morten Morland
The Times

During a speech outside Number 10, David Cameron urged voters to give him a chance to finish the job of 'turning our country around', insisting that 'Britain is back on its feet again'. Earlier in the week, during a TV interview with Jeremy Paxman, Cameron had been forced to admit that he did not know how many food banks existed in the UK. Paxman provided the answer for him, revealing that the number of food banks had risen from 66 to 421 since Cameron had first come to office.

31 March 2015
Peter Brookes
The Times

Whilst touring a Cardiff brewery, David Cameron said that the message he wished to send to Welsh voters was: 'the plan's working – stick with the plan, stick with the team.' A fortnight earlier, during his final cabinet meeting, Cameron had given out bottles of the 4.5% 'Co-ale-ition' IPA made by Wychwood Brewery – a small company located in the heart of his Oxfordshire constituency. The ale was described as having notes of oak and zesty lemon, and was recommended for 'unconventional pairing'. It was specially commissioned by Cameron for the meeting and produced in a limited run of 50 bottles.

2 April 2015
Steve Bell
Guardian

'Opportunity knocks! Ed Miliband thinks it's time we had a female James Bond. Vote for us and it could be you!'

Ed Miliband revealed during a radio interview that, in addition to his better-known policies, he was also campaigning for the first female James Bond. After meeting Rosamund Pike at the Magic Radio studios, the Labour leader tipped her to make history by becoming the first woman in the role, saying: 'I think she's a great British actress, she'd make a great Bond. This is 2015, I think we can move with the times.'

2 April 2015
Stan McMurtry
Daily Mail

According to the cartoonist: 'It was assumed that we were heading for a hung parliament and that either Cameron or Miliband would have to be propped up by smaller parties in order to become leader. So here we have the two potential leaders in an Easter colouring-in game, depicted as eggs (both of them seem to suit egg form quite nicely) and surrounded by pencils resembling the different parties that would be used to colour in the chosen leader. As we know now, this didn't turn out to be the case and now we have a completely Tory blue egg in charge, but how long before he cracks . . . ?'

4 April 2015
Ben Jennings
i

According to the cartoonist: '*The Voice* final was to be held that night, a few days after the first of the leaders' debates on TV. The one was the usual cacophonous nonsense with a bunch of over-achieving narcissists vying for attention. The other was . . . *The Voice* final. (Boom tish!) The poor voter/viewer could be excused for feeling a little nightmarish existential angst.'

5 April 2015
Andy Davey
Sun on Sunday

5 April 2015
Peter Schrank
Independent on Sunday

According to the cartoonist: 'Cartoons which feature more than two or three caricatures are always daunting. Especially if some of them are women, who are generally more difficult to caricature than men. Also if it's your first attempt with some of them, as was the case here with Natalie Bennett and Leanne Wood. And it's difficult to give them all something to do, as well as arranging them in an interesting composition.'

In a reported meeting between Nicola Sturgeon and the French ambassador, the SNP leader was alleged to have said she preferred David Cameron to Ed Miliband. According to the cartoonist: 'This was a gag I thought of immediately but then worried it was either too obvious or too reliant on people remembering the advert. The hardest element was getting the Ferrero Rocher wrappers to look right.'

5 April 2015
Bob Moran
Daily Telegraph

6 April 2015
Morten Morland
The Times

Major changes to UK pension rules came into force on Easter Monday, with George Osborne hailing the moves as 'a revolution' and 'the biggest changes to pensions in 100 years'. Under the new rules, those aged 55 and over with defined-contribution pensions can now decide what to do with their retirement savings. Osborne summarised the policy by saying: 'What it means is that people who have worked hard and saved hard can have access to their pensions savings.'

According to the cartoonist: 'I'd been fairly gentle on UKIP so far, focusing more on the Tories' discomfort, but suddenly there was a poll saying that Nigel Farage might not even win his own proposed seat in Thanet. It was time to stick it to him.'

6 April 2015
Christian Adams
Daily Telegraph

THE GHOST OF ELECTIONS PAST...

8 April 2015
Dave Brown
Independent

According to the cartoonist: 'Tony Blair made a surprise intervention in the election campaign. But would his support be a help or a hindrance to Ed Miliband?'

ALL BEHIND YOU, DAVE

AFTER *Low*

David Cameron dismissed Miliband's plans to scrap the non-domiciles tax loophole, describing Labour's stance on the matter as one of 'total chaos and confusion'. Subsequent YouGov polls suggested clear public support for Labour's policy, leading Cameron's opponents to seize on his remarks as evidence of the Tories being out of touch with regard to the interests of the less well-off. Bell's response is a pastiche of David Low's 1940 cartoon, 'All behind you, Winston', featuring Churchill leading the wartime all-party coalition.

9 April 2015
Steve Bell
Guardian

Defence Secretary Michael Fallon claimed that Ed Miliband's failure to commit to renewing Britain's nuclear deterrent suggested the Labour leader would be prepared to 'barter away' Trident in exchange for a post-election pact with the SNP. In a strange and highly personal attack, Fallon compared the situation to Miliband's decision to stand against his brother in the Labour leadership race in 2010, saying: 'Ed Miliband stabbed his own brother in the back to become Labour leader. Now he is willing to stab the United Kingdom in the back to become prime minister.'

10 April 2015
Peter Brookes
The Times

As he unveiled the Conservatives' election manifesto, David Cameron said that his aim was to guarantee a 'good life' for British workers and families. The prime minister pledged to keep minimum wage workers out of the income tax system, to double free childcare to 30 hours a week and to extend Thatcher's 'right to buy' scheme to 1.3 million housing association tenants. In response to Cameron's apparent reference to the 1970s sitcom, *The Good Life*, Labour dubbed the Tories the 'Margo and Jerry' of British politics.

15 April 2015
Peter Brookes
The Times

AND THE WINNER IS...

DEBATE

ADAMS 5
17.4.

17 April 2015
Christian Adams
Daily Telegraph

David Cameron and Nick Clegg were conspicuously absent from the second TV debate of the general election campaign, in which Ed Miliband came under concerted attack from Scottish and Welsh nationalists. The prime minister had declined to take part, leading the BBC to exclude the deputy PM as well.

According to the cartoonist: 'After the so called "Opposition" debate on 16 April where Nicola Sturgeon offered a post-election deal to Labour, Ed Miliband ruled it out – but the prospect of becoming prime minister with the SNP's help must have been tempting. The Trident submarine floating in the loch behind them is a reminder of the policy differences between them.'

19 April 2015
Dave Simonds
Observer

HERE BE MONSTERS...

22 April 2015
Dave Brown
Independent

According to the cartoonist: 'John Major attempted to portray possible SNP support for a Labour government as a dire threat to the UK. Meanwhile, Google celebrated the 81st anniversary of the famously hoaxed photo of Nessie.'

RESCUE MISSION

Hundreds of migrants drowned in the Mediterranean amid a surge in overcrowded boats heading for Europe from Libya. Italy urged its EU partners to do more to help with the growing crisis. According to the cartoonist: 'EU leaders agreed to send ships and funds to restore rescue operations in the Mediterranean after the deaths of almost a thousand migrants. David Cameron insisted that any refugees rescued by British ships would be landed in Italy, not the UK.'

25 April 2015
Ingram Pinn
Financial Times

David Cameron and Boris Johnson warned of an impending 'constitutional crisis' in reaction to footage from an SNP candidate event in which Alex Salmond joked that he would be writing Labour's budget. In response to Cameron's warning, Salmond said the prime minister should 'try holding a few public meetings and meeting real people', and described him as having 'both a people bypass and a sense of humour bypass'. Meanwhile, the Tory party chairman, Grant Shapps, was accused of editing Wikipedia pages to promote himself at the expense of his political rivals.

26 April 2015
Chris Riddell
Observer

After facing criticism from Tory donors for 'a serious lack of energy and belief in his campaign', Cameron gave a speech at the Institute of Chartered Accountants in which he insisted he was 'pumped up' and 'bloody lively'. In his address to the small business leaders gathered for the event, Cameron bellowed, 'Taking a risk! Having a punt! Having a go! That pumps me up . . . We have got a fight on our hands and I am going to win that fight.'

28 April 2015
Steve Bell
Guardian

30 April 2015
Christian Adams
Daily Telegraph

Ed Miliband came under fire for being interviewed by comedian Russell Brand. Miliband said he was attempting to reach out to the hundreds of thousands of young people who follow Brand. But Conservatives criticised him for his lack of judgement, given Brand's stance against voting in elections. The same week, David Cameron had unveiled a five-year 'tax lock' policy which would guarantee no increases in the rates of income tax, VAT or national insurance before May 2020.

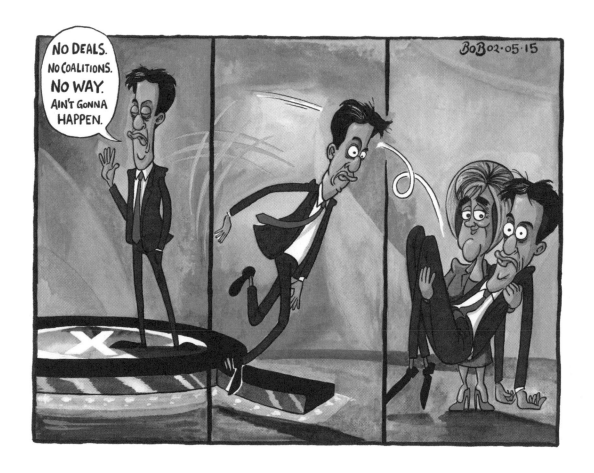

Following Ed Miliband's appearance on the BBC *Question Time* leaders' election special he tripped while walking off the stage. According to the cartoonist: 'I watched Miliband trip and knew I had to try and use it for a cartoon. With this sort of joke, sometimes it takes a while to figure out how many boxes or cels you need to make it work best. You also have the restriction of the shape of your space in the paper. Three side by side worked well because it meant I could show Miliband's long gangly frame.'

2 May 2015
Bob Moran
Daily Telegraph

4 May 2015
Martin Rowson
Guardian

Not surprisingly, following the announcement of the birth of Princess Charlotte, Britain's leading politicians took time out from the election campaign to send William and Kate their best wishes. The Conservatives were particularly keen to draw attention to the event, hoping that a national sense of well-being might boost their share of the vote.

GOVERN WITHOUT ME AND YOU'RE DOOMED!!

Nick Clegg warned that there would be a second general election 'before Christmas' if either Labour or the Tories tried to form a minority government after 7 May. He argued that only another 'strong and stable' coalition involving his party could save the country, saying: 'The great risk of not having the Liberal Democrats in Parliament, in government, is we lurch off into this blue-KIP alliance between David Cameron, UKIP, the DUP and the rest of them cutting, cutting, cutting way beyond what's necessary, or reckless borrowing as Ed Miliband and Alex Salmond are in some kind of deathly embrace on the left.'

6 May 2015
Steve Bell
Guardian

7 May 2015
Christian Adams
Daily Telegraph

As the election campaign drew to a close, it was widely believed that Britain was heading for the second hung parliament in succession, with preliminary results of the final ICM/Guardian campaign poll suggesting that Labour and the Conservatives were tied at 35% each.

MOVING BACK IN...

10

CHAMPAGN

BEN-JENNINGS.COM

According to the cartoonist: 'This cartoon was produced on the morning after the election when it became clear that despite widespread predictions of a hung parliament, the Tories had won by a narrow majority. I depicted Cameron with Samantha moving back into Downing Street, followed by a box full of sharp objects (among other Tory clichés in the back of the van). It was ominous that the Conservatives, without the Lib Dems around to restrain them, would now introduce massive cuts to meet their deficit reduction programme.'

9 May 2015
Ben Jennings
i

LABOUR ISN'T WORKING.

UNEMPLOYMENT OFFICE

BOB 09·05·15

According to the cartoonist: 'I was hesitant about using this idea because I felt that there had been quite a lot of other cartoons based on this election poster [run by the Conservatives in the build-up to the 1979 general election]. There was so much happening on that day that I wasn't sure if this would be a good image to summarise the election aftermath. By late afternoon, when I'd finished it and the dust had started to settle, I felt much more satisfied that it did the job.'

9 May 2015
Bob Moran
Daily Telegraph

After David Cameron's surprise election victory, Eurosceptic Conservative MPs immediately put him under pressure to gain major concessions when renegotiating the terms of Britain's EU membership. Their demands included reforms to the EU's freedom of movement rules and allowing the UK Parliament to veto EU laws.

10 May 2015
Chris Riddell
Observer

A PERIOD OF REFLECTION...

11 May 2015
Morten Morland
The Times

Despite many in the Labour Party demanding a swift leadership contest following the resignation of Ed Miliband, Shadow Education Secretary Tristram Hunt, himself a potential candidate, called for a period of reflection. Among others tipped to enter the contest were Chuka Umunna, Liz Kendall and Dan Jarvis, all of whom had been in the House of Commons for five years or less.

In a sign of the Conservatives' gradual regression to the right since David Cameron's first conference speech as leader, in which he urged the party to 'let sunshine win the day', Cameron appointed Iain Duncan Smith as Work and Pensions Secretary. The former Tory leader's new role meant that the man who had presided over the 'bedroom tax' and the £26,000 benefits cap would now be in charge of making the extensive benefit cuts the Tories had promised in their election manifesto.

12 May 2015
Steve Bell
Guardian

Culture and Media Secretary Sajid Javid accused the BBC of bias, suggesting that the corporation 'could have done a more balanced job' in its coverage of the election campaign. Javid cited one particular episode of the *Today* programme as being 'very, very anti-Tory'. Earlier in the campaign, Conservative MP Andrew Bridgen had also complained about the audience composition for the *Question Time* leaders' debate. Bridgen felt that there was an unfair proportion of Labour and Lib Dem voters in the audience, describing this perceived imbalance as confirming 'the unashamed left-wing bias of the BBC'.

13 May 2015
Christian Adams
Daily Telegraph

David Cameron and Nicola Sturgeon met in Edinburgh for their first talks since the election. Sturgeon described the meeting as 'constructive', saying that the two had agreed to progress as planned with proposals for further devolution, though they continued to clash over the extent to which Scotland will be able to control its tax and spending policies. This cartoon is a pastiche of David Low's 1939 cartoon on the Nazi–Soviet division of Poland featuring Hitler and Stalin.

16 May 2015
Martin Rowson
Guardian

17 May 2015
Peter Schrank
Independent on Sunday

Nigel Farage remained leader of UKIP after his resignation was rejected by the party's national executive committee. According to the cartoonist: 'As a voter and as a UK citizen I was hoping we'd seen the last of Nigel Farage; as a cartoonist I was delighted when he so unexpectedly bounced back. Which highlights the dilemma we cartoonists often face: we rely on bad news and controversial, unpleasant politicians for our inspiration and motivation.'

Len McCluskey, the general secretary of Unite, warned that his union's affiliation to Labour could be reconsidered if it thought the party's next leader failed to represent working people. In a BBC interview, McCluskey refused to be drawn on his preferred leadership candidate but said it was 'essential that the correct leader emerged'.

18 May 2015
Morten Morland
The Times

25 May 2015
Martin Rowson
Guardian

In a historic referendum, the Republic of Ireland voted by a huge majority to amend the country's constitution to legalise same-sex marriage, so becoming the first country in the world to do so by popular vote. The result was hailed as a triumph of progressive thinking by the mainstream media and the political establishment. Meanwhile, the Conservatives were considering holding a parliamentary vote on repealing the fox-hunting ban.

Acting leader Harriet Harman said that Labour would now support plans for an EU referendum by the end of 2017. According to the cartoonist: 'Labour doing a U-turn almost by accident because of the amount of people trying to drive the car really appealed as an idea. I enjoyed putting a demented Blair in the back seat. Liz Kendall's finger up Andy Burnham's nose was a late alteration suggested by my editor.'

25 May 2015
Bob Moran
Daily Telegraph

27 May 2015
Christian Adams
Daily Telegraph

Germany and France agreed a pact to create a closer political union between member states of the eurozone without the need for treaty change. The agreement between Merkel and Hollande could restrict David Cameron's plans for EU reform ahead of a referendum on Britain's membership.

According to the cartoonist: 'After numerous charges of racketeering, fraud, money laundering and bribery were levelled at FIFA, its president, Sepp Blatter, still got re-elected for a further five years. FIFA seems to be going down the pan, so that's how I portrayed it.'

31 May 2015
Dave Simonds
Observer

5 June 2015
Steve Bell
Guardian

George Osborne prepared the ground for an expected £12 billion of welfare cuts in his upcoming budget, describing Britain's current welfare spending as 'unsustainable'. Earlier in June, four people had been seriously injured at Alton Towers when their carriage on the Smiler ride collided with another that had come to a halt on the track.

THE LONE RANGER...

Barack Obama urged David Cameron to ensure that Britain maintained its NATO spending target. The US president warned the prime minister against cutting the UK defence budget, stating that a failure to hit the spending target of 2% of GDP would risk undermining the military alliance.

8 June 2015
Christian Adams
Daily Telegraph

149

The Eurosceptic 'Conservatives for Britain' group, launched on 7 June, claimed that up to nine Tory cabinet ministers could support a vote for the UK to leave the EU in the upcoming referendum. The group, chaired by Steve Baker MP, raised the bar on the renegotiation of Britain's membership, warning that they would campaign to leave the EU unless Cameron was able to win the reforms they wanted.

8 June 2015
Brian Adcock
Independent

David Cameron denied stating that ministers would be forced to resign if they failed to back him in the EU referendum. At the start of the G7 summit in Germany, Cameron had said: 'If you want to be part of the government you have to take the view that we are engaged in an exercise of renegotiation and that will lead to a successful outcome . . . Everyone in government is signed up to the programme set out in the Conservative manifesto.' Cameron later complained that his comments had been 'misinterpreted' and that he had been referring only to the process of renegotiation, not to the vote itself.

9 June 2015
Morten Morland
The Times

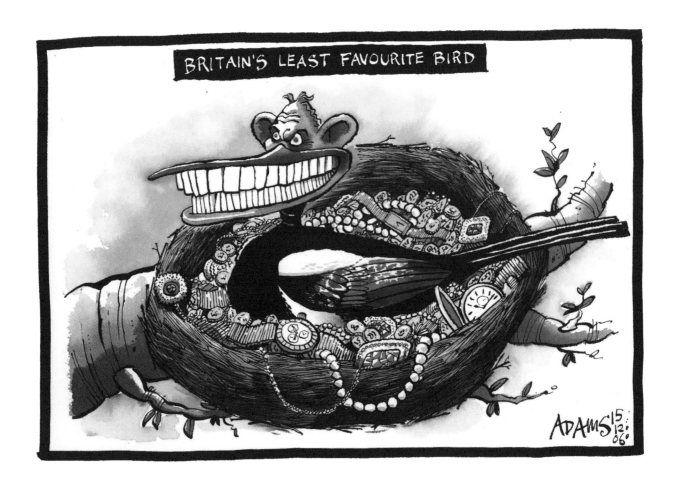

BRITAIN'S LEAST FAVOURITE BIRD

ADAMS 15/12/06

12 June 2015
Christian Adams
Daily Telegraph

Tony Blair was accused of a possible conflict of interest after documents were seen by the *Telegraph* which appeared to indicate that the former prime minister had used identical trips to conduct both private business meetings and talks in his capacity as Middle East peace envoy. The *Telegraph* calculated that these trips could incur a potential cost to the taxpayer of some £16,000 a week. Meanwhile, a nationwide poll revealed that the robin was Britain's favourite bird.

David Cameron was criticised by civil liberties campaigners after using a speech on the 800th anniversary of Magna Carta to signal his intention to go ahead with plans to abolish the Human Rights Act. During a ceremony at Runnymede Green, where King John added his seal to the historic document in 1215, Cameron alluded to the government's plans to replace the European convention on human rights with a British bill of rights. The director of Liberty, Shami Chakrabarti, described Cameron's speech as 'a masterclass in bare-faced cheek', while Yvette Cooper accused him of trying to 'hijack' the event for political means.

16 June 2015
Steve Bell
Guardian

16 June 2015
Dave Brown
Independent

The left-winger Jeremy Corbyn became the fourth candidate in the Labour leadership election after securing the 35 nominations required to stand. Corbyn, considered the only anti-austerity candidate, joined Andy Burnham, Yvette Cooper and Liz Kendall in the contest.

The Conservatives decided to end subsidies to onshore windfarms from 1 April 2016, a year earlier than originally planned in the agreement drawn up by the Tory–Liberal Democrat coalition. Former energy and climate change secretary Ed Davey condemned the move, saying: 'Anti-wind power Tories will put up electricity bills, cut green jobs and reduce investment.'

19 June 2015
Christian Adams
Daily Telegraph

20 June 2015
Morten Morland
The Times

At the St Petersburg Economic Forum, Alexis Tsipras raised the possibility of Greece forming an alliance with Russia if his country exited the eurozone. Putin's deputy prime minister, Arkady Dvorkovich, responded by saying: 'The most important things for us are investment projects and trade with Greece. If financial support is needed, we will consider this question.'

On 17 June in Charleston, South Carolina, 21-year-old white supremacist Dylann Roof shot and killed nine people at one of the oldest black churches in the US. According to the cartoonist: 'This is a cartoon that doesn't contain any joke or seek to make any real criticism. It is more about trying to crystallise a political situation. The expectation that Obama would be the president to end racial tensions in America; the legacy of Martin Luther King; the problem of gun control. I wanted a simple way to illustrate a complicated tragedy.'

20 June 2015
Bob Moran
Daily Telegraph

According to the cartoonist: 'Iain Duncan Smith and George Osborne were apparently harmonious in their plans to go ahead with £12 billion in welfare cuts. This was the day after a quarter of a million attended an anti-austerity march in London that included a speech from Russell Brand amongst others (hence his inclusion). I was struck by the timing of the newspaper articles. It was as if Osborne and IDS, who must have been aware the march was happening that weekend, were saying "Sod you lot, march all you want, we can do whatever we want!"'

22 June 2015
Brian Adcock
Independent

David Cameron confirmed that the government would be pushing ahead with the planned £12 billion of welfare cuts. In a speech in Runcorn, the prime minister suggested that much of the money would come from cutting tax credits and housing benefit, promising an end to what he described as the 'ridiculous merry-go-round' of taxing people in low-paid jobs, then handing them money back in benefits.

23 June 2015
Morten Morland
The Times

25 June 2015
Morten Morland
The Times

There were Channel Tunnel delays after around 150 migrants tried to storm the terminal in Calais in a bid to board UK-bound lorries and trains. David Cameron told European Union leaders he accepted it might be impossible to change the EU's governing treaty before an in–out referendum on the UK's membership in the bloc.

BoB 28·06·15

According to the cartoonist: 'For the terrorist attack on British holidaymakers in Tunisia, I tried to do something poignant but also with an element of defiance. The idea of the sandcastle was to show innocence, but also how vulnerable we now seem to be to this type of attack. Nevertheless, it's still standing and the flag is still flying. I thought it would be interesting to do such a bright, colourful image that carried such a sombre message.'

28 June 2015
Bob Moran
Daily Telegraph

ANOTHER CLOSED ATM...

€UROBANK

The European Central Bank froze emergency lending to Greek banks after eurozone finance ministers refused to extend Greece's bailout programme to allow the country to hold a referendum over the terms of a new deal. In response, Tsipras ordered Greece's banks to close and imposed a daily limit of €60 on cash withdrawals from ATMs. Long lines of people queued outside banks as it was reported that cash machines were running out of money.

30 June 2015
Dave Brown
Independent

After the Airports Commission recommended that a third runway be built at Heathrow, David Cameron announced that the government would make a decision on the matter by the end of the year. Boris Johnson responded by saying that any expansion of Heathrow would be 'catastrophic', leading Labour's acting leader Harriet Harman to ask whether Cameron would 'stand up for Britain's interests' or 'just be bullied by Boris'.

2 July 2015
Dave Brown
Independent

4 July 2015
Martin Rowson
Guardian

As part of controversial new plans to reduce costs in the NHS, Jeremy Hunt announced that, from 2016, prescription medicines costing more than £20 would be labelled with their indicative costs to the NHS and marked 'funded by taxpayers'. Hunt said that patients needed to take 'more personal responsibility for use of precious public resources . . . We spend £300 million a year on wasted medicines. People who use our services need to know that in the end they pay the price for this waste.'

George Osborne announced major cuts to welfare spending in his summer budget. Amongst these were a four-year freeze on benefits for working-age people (excluding maternity and disability payments); the scrapping of the automatic entitlement to housing benefit for 18–21-year-olds; and the restriction of child tax credits so that families would no longer be able to claim additional support for more than two children. Osborne said: 'The benefits system should not support lifestyles and rents that are not available to the taxpayers who pay for that system.'

5 July 2015
Chris Riddell
Observer

GESTURE of RESPECT

GESTURE POLITICS

RAF

5 July 2015
Peter Schrank
Independent on Sunday

According to the cartoonist: 'We're familiar with seeing the bodies of soldiers killed in Afghanistan being carried off RAF transport planes in Brize Norton. When the victims of the beach attacks in Tunisia were repatriated in the same way I felt moved by the dignity of the occasion, but uneasy to see them treated as if they were combatants in some foreign war. When the government started talking about another vote in Parliament on attacking Syria, as a response to the murders, then my feelings of unease were confirmed.'

Despite a collapsing economy, 61% of Greek voters rejected the European Commission, International Monetary Fund and European Central Bank's proposed bailout terms in a national referendum. Angela Merkel was now under greater pressure than ever to resolve the Greek imbroglio.

7 July 2015
Christian Adams
Daily Telegraph

11 July 2015
Scott Clissold
Sunday Express

Prince Philip was caught on camera swearing at a photographer during a photocall at an event marking the 75th anniversary of the Battle of Britain. The Duke of Edinburgh grew impatient as he waited for a group photograph to be taken and was filmed saying: 'Just take the fucking picture.'

George Osborne sought to outflank Labour by making a big rise in the minimum wage the centrepiece of his budget. According to the cartoonist: 'The predictability and annual repetition of the budget makes it a somewhat dull subject for cartoons. This year it had strong political and strategic implications and therefore was more interesting than usual. And it coincided with Wimbledon, which gave me a chance to break away from the usual imagery of red boxes, rabbits out of hats, axes and other cutting implements.'

12 July 2015
Peter Schrank
Independent on Sunday

14 July 2015
Ben Jennings
Independent

According to the cartoonist: 'This image of a handshake represents the deal between eurozone leaders and Greece (identified by their cufflinks), on a third bailout agreement for Greece and its collapsing economy. The deal is to come at a heavy price, however, with a stringent austerity package attached to it: the sort which the leading party in Greece, Syriza, had campaigned vehemently against. I depicted people squeezed within the handshake to represent the Greek people who are the ones that will feel the pain of these further austerity measures that have already ravaged their country.'

THE UNMANAGEABLE IN PURSUIT OF THE INEVITABLE...

Nicola Sturgeon told David Cameron he was 'not master of all he surveys' after the SNP forced the government to postpone a vote on relaxing fox-hunting laws in England and Wales. Earlier in the year, Sturgeon had said: 'The SNP have a longstanding position of not voting on matters that purely affect England – such as fox-hunting south of the border, for example – and we stand by that.' Cameron described the SNP's U-turn as 'entirely opportunistic'. Adams's cartoon on the matter pays tribute to the much-loved cartoonist Norman Thelwell.

15 July 2015
Christian Adams
Daily Telegraph

17 July 2015
Dave Brown
Independent

Two private polls conducted on behlaf of Jeremy Corbyn's opponents put him in the lead for the Labour leadership. Corbyn had been expected to finish last in the contest, having only secured the 35 nominations required to stand at the last minute. A surge in support for the veteran left-winger led Ladbrokes to cut its odds on his chance of victory to 5/1, having started him on 100/1 when he joined the race.

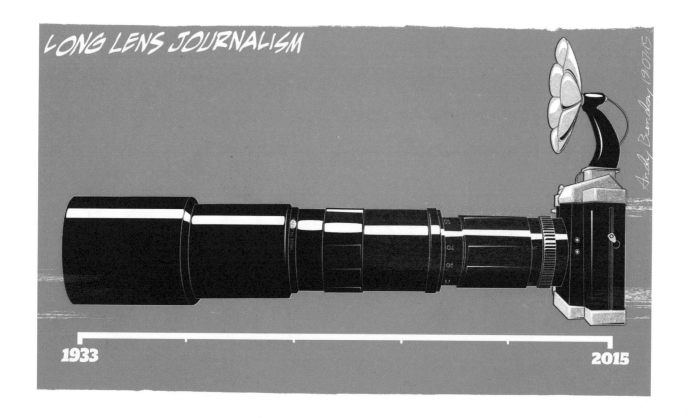

The *Sun* published film footage from 1933 which showed the Queen – then aged six or seven – performing a Nazi salute with her mother, sister and uncle on the lawn in the gardens of Balmoral. Buckingham Palace said it was 'disappointing that film shot eight decades ago had been obtained and exploited'.

19 July 2015
Andy Bunday
Independent on Sunday

19 July 2015
Bob Moran
Daily Telegraph

According to the cartoonist: 'The papers were full of stories about seagull attacks. Originally, I wanted to do something with Cameron being "bombed" by seagulls and link it to UK pilots bombing terrorists in Syria. Then I realised it would be funnier to have the seagulls attacking the terrorists. I think people enjoy cartoons that mix two vastly different subjects. And there's something amusingly ridiculous about a member of ISIS eating fish and chips in the desert.'

Acting leader Harriet Harman said that Labour would not vote against the government's welfare bill, including the limiting of child tax credits to two children. Harman urged Labour MPs to abstain on the bill, despite vocal opposition from within the party. Bell's cartoon is based on a Nazi poster advertising the benefits of saving for 'your own KdF car'. This referred to the Kraft durch Freude ('Strength Through Joy') organisation which produced the KdF-Wagen – later known as the Volkswagen Beetle.

22 July 2015
Steve Bell
Guardian

26 July 2015
Chris Riddell
Observer

Labour leadership outsider Liz Kendall refused to bow to pressure to step aside and reduce the threat from Jeremy Corbyn by allowing her supporters to switch to Cooper or Burnham. A YouGov poll had put Corbyn 17 points ahead of Burnham on first preferences, whilst Kendall was last on 11%.

According to the cartoonist: 'When Labour leadership candidate Jeremy Corbyn was asked by Andrew Marr if he was a Marxist he didn't deny it, and he has said if he were to become prime minister he would renationalise the railways. The cartoon shows Corbyn in Karl Marx pose, playing on the famous Marx quote: "You have nothing to lose but your chains."'

27 July 2015
Gary Barker
The Times

28 July 2015
Christian Adams
Daily Telegraph

Labour peer Lord Sewel resigned from the House of Lords after being filmed allegedly taking drugs with prostitutes. Footage appeared to show the former deputy speaker of the Lords snorting powder from a woman's breasts, while in a later video he was shown wearing an orange bra and making disparaging remarks about a number of senior politicians. Sewel apologised for the 'pain and embarrassment' he had caused his family and said his resignation would 'limit and help repair' the damage to the reputation of the Lords.

According to the cartoonist: 'After a fatal accident amid the chaos at the Calais terminal, Cameron confirmed extra funding for new fencing to keep migrants away from the tunnel, saying that the situation was "very concerning". Meanwhile, George Osborne, who will help lead Britain's attempt to renegotiate key EU treaties, advised that Britain should return to a "trade relationship" with the EU. This sounded considerably more strident than Cameron's renegotiating position. Was Osborne positioning himself to succeed Cameron after the 2017 referendum?'

30 July 2015
Andy Davey
Independent

According to the cartoonist: 'This was one of those great opportunities to summarise a news story with just a simple image. The cartoon is about Jeremy Clarkson signing a deal with Amazon, but it also refers to the wider situation of the BBC looking increasingly redundant in the face of video streaming services. Purists would argue that it's not really a political cartoon but, in my defence, all the politicians were on holiday.'

1 August 2015
Bob Moran
Daily Telegraph

According to the cartoonist: 'The cartoon refers to revelations that one in seven athletes whose blood was tested for doping between 2001 and 2012 had highly suspect results, and some of these were Olympic medal winners.'

3 August 2015
Gary Barker
The Times

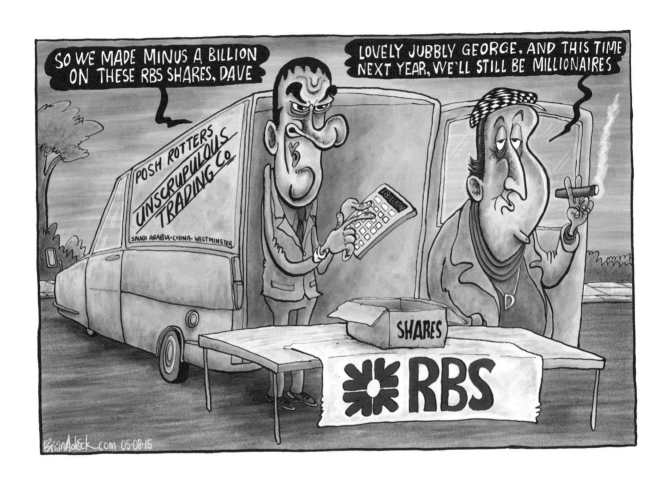

According to the cartoonist: 'This cartoon was in the *Guardian* and judging by the shares it seemed people liked it. I think what people enjoyed is the comparison between the lovable, working-class Rodney and Derek Trotter, forever dreaming of being millionaires, and the ridiculously posh duo of Cameron and Osborne with actual millions and their hideous sense of entitlement. I did worry slightly that it might make Dave and George appear more human, but it would take a lot more than a mere cartoon to do that.'

5 August 2015
Brian Adcock
Guardian

In their ongoing dispute with London Underground over proposals for a new night service, unions organised a series of 24-hour tube strikes. Boris Johnson criticised the walkouts, stating that they would leave millions of commuters facing travel disruption. In an interview with BBC News, a long-serving tube driver said: 'We get paid an amazing salary and the holidays are great too [43 days' leave including eight bank holidays] but why should I be forced to work nights and more weekends when that is not what I signed up for? It's about the principle of changing our working conditions without discussions.'

7 August 2015
Dave Brown
Independent

BALANCED DEBATE

8 August 2015
Ingram Pinn
Financial Times

According to the cartoonist: 'A TV debate between ten of the 16 Republican candidates for the nomination for US president was dominated by the egomaniacal and buffoonish billionaire Donald Trump, who astonishingly has taken the lead of an increasingly right-wing field.'

Jeremy Corbyn suggested that Labour should consider reinstating clause four of the party's constitution, which was seen by many as committing the party to renationalisation. His statements drew criticism from party members who saw Blair's abolition of the old clause four as playing a crucial part in persuading voters to elect a Labour government.

10 August 2015
Martin Rowson
Guardian

13 August 2015
Morten Morland
The Times

Democratic presidential candidate Hillary Clinton denied claims that she had sent classified emails through her private server while she was secretary of state, saying: 'I am confident that I never sent nor received any information that was classified at the time.' However, investigators from the State Department issued a report indicating that at least 60 emails sent through the server had contained classified data.

According to the cartoonist: 'The "cliffs of doom" cliché is one of the most overused in cartooning, but I overcame my reservations because the image works well and I liked the idea of Corbyn in the caravan. The three slick and hapless candidates, in spite of their blandness, are actually fun to draw, as is Corbyn. A beard always helps. I'm not altogether sure if I see the situation quite as starkly as portrayed here. I think I agree with Germaine Greer. She suggested on BBC 4's *Any Questions?* that Corbyn was not running to be prime minister, but leader of the opposition, and that he might be better at opposing than the other candidates. However it turns out, with Corbyn leading Labour, politics and political cartooning will get a lot more interesting.'

16 August 2015
Peter Schrank
Independent on Sunday

According to the cartoonist: 'Cameron urged Chilcot to "get on with it" and publish the Iraq Inquiry, now six years into its preparation. Delays had been caused by the "Maxwellisation" process, which gives individuals facing possible criticism the opportunity to respond before publication. There is politics afoot here, of course. Those who wish to delay its publication are likely to be Blair and his cadre – who have presumably been "Maxwellising" with vigour. This means that Cameron can occupy the moral high ground and demand publication with impunity.'

17 August 2015
Andy Davey
Independent

Gordon Brown became the latest senior Labour figure to try to steer voters away from choosing Jeremy Corbyn as the party's next leader. In a speech at London's Royal Festival Hall, the former prime minister did not refer to any of the Labour leadership candidates by name but made a thinly veiled allusion to his distrust of Corbyn's foreign policy, saying: 'Don't tell me that we can do much for the poor of the world if the alliances we favour most are with Hezbollah, Hamas, Chávez's successor in Venezuela and Putin's totalitarian Russia.'

17 August 2015
Christian Adams
Daily Telegraph

19 August 2015
Morten Morland
The Times

Former Labour leader Ed Miliband faced growing hostility from colleagues who blamed him for a change in the electoral rules that assisted Jeremy Corbyn into pole position. Miliband changed the system under which he was elected to 'one member, one vote' and allowed the public to take part for a £3 fee. One member of the shadow cabinet described the change as 'mad' and 'a terrible mistake'. Miliband, who was on holiday in Australia at the time, was the only senior Labour party figure not to comment on the leadership election.

According to the cartoonist: 'Forget the general election, the Labour party, the crisis in Greece: this is the subject of the year. Not least because it's connected with so many other important issues: the worldwide contrast between poverty and wealth; globalisation; chaos in the Middle East and the Maghreb; the rise of militant Islam; and climate change. I don't find it an easy area for cartoons. Humour can feel inappropriate. On the other hand, trying to come up with ever more grim imagery to describe misery can leave me feeling self-indulgent, smug even.'

23 August 2015
Peter Schrank
Independent on Sunday

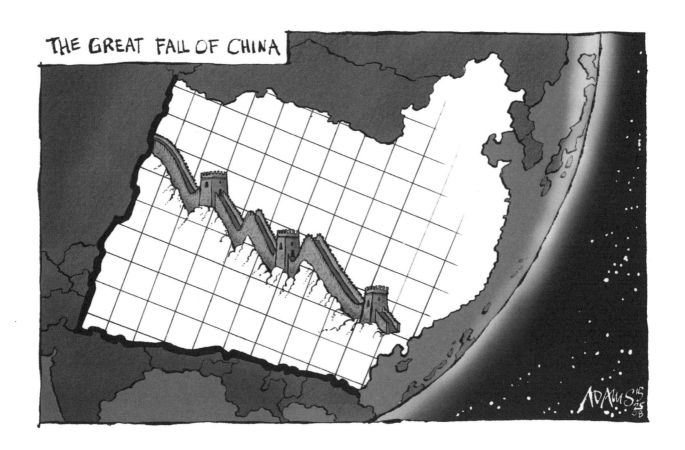

THE GREAT FALL OF CHINA

25 August 2015
Christian Adams
Daily Telegraph

Stock markets across the world fell sharply as global investors reacted to fears of a Chinese economic slowdown. The Dow plummeted a staggering 1089 points, its biggest ever points drop. One floor trader said the US markets were 'bordering on the edge of panic'.

Harriet Harman stated that 3,000 alleged 'cheats' were excluded from voting in the Labour leadership contest because they did not share the party's aims and values. Harman denied suggestions the party was 'purging' Jeremy Corbyn's supporters, thousands of whom are thought to have signed up to vote for him.

26 August 2015
Steve Bell
Guardian

Net migration to the UK reached an all-time high of 330,000 in the year ending March 2015 – a figure more than three times higher than the government's own target. Nigel Farage described the increase as reflecting a 'borderless' Britain and again called on the prime minister to make immigration a focal point of the upcoming renegotiation of Britain's membership of the EU. Meanwhile, David Cameron also faced criticism for appointing 45 new peers, including 26 former Tory ministers and aides, taking the total membership of the House of Lords to 826.

28 August 2015
Morten Morland
The Times